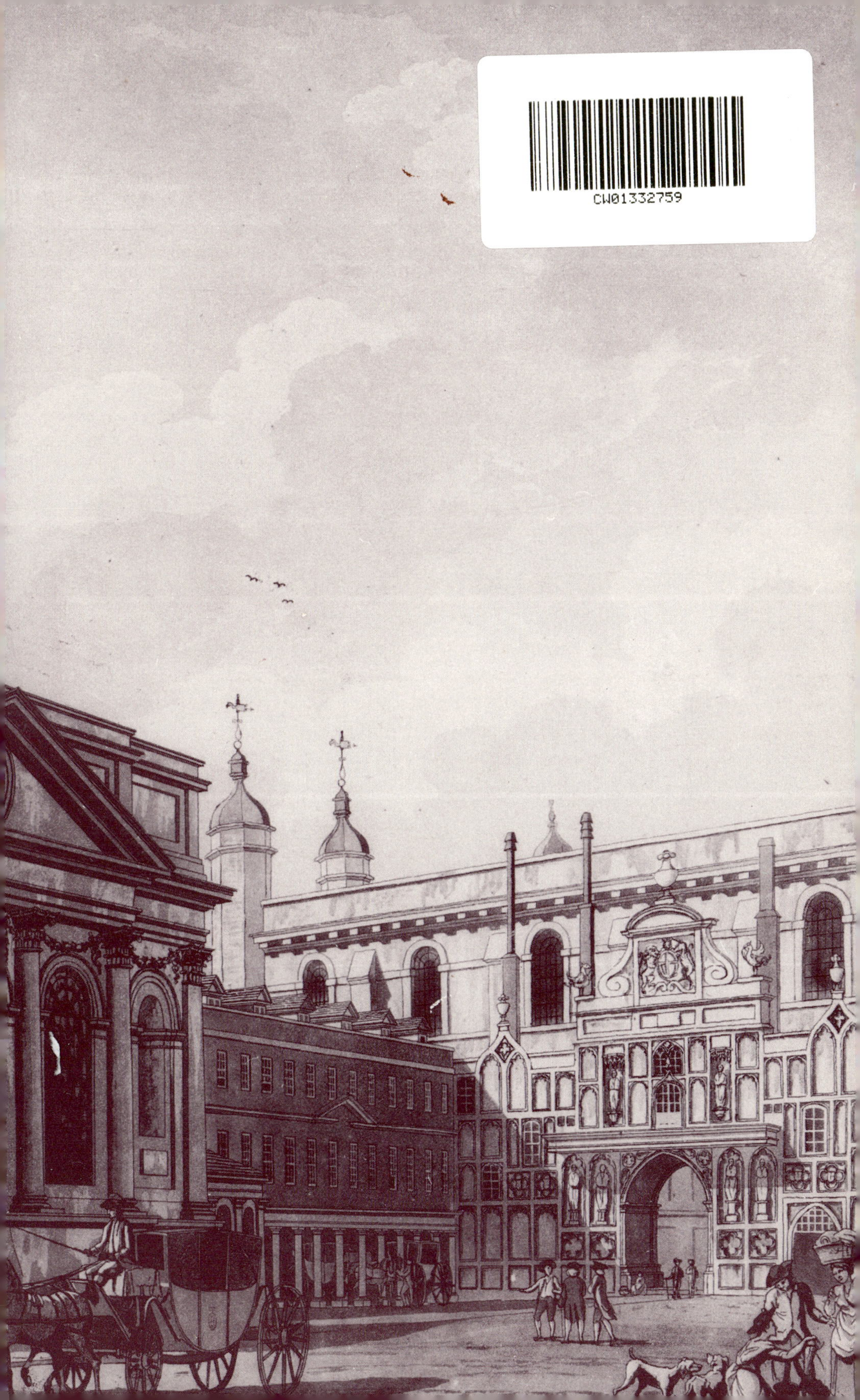

Airs & Graces

Airs & Graces

BASIL WATSON

With the best wishes of the author

Basil Watson

LONDON
1993

© 1993 by Basil Watson

All rights reserved. No part of this
publication may be reproduced, stored
in a retrieval system, or transmitted,
in any form, or by any means,
electronic, mechanical, photocopying,
recording or otherwise without the
prior permission of the
copyright owner.

ISBN 0 9510904 1 0

Ashburnham Publishers
19 Straightsmouth
Greenwich
London SE10 9LB

First published 1993

Printed in Great Britain by
Henry Ling Ltd
The Dorset Press, Dorchester, Dorset

*To my ever generous wife, Janibel,
who never begrudged me the many evenings out
that these Graces imply;
and to our grand-daughter, Andrina,
who cheerfully volunteered for the task of
dealing with my longhand
and was immensely relieved when she found
just how much a word processor helped.*

ACKNOWLEDGEMENTS

The author acknowledges the generous help of many friends not least of Ann Murray, my literary agent, and Vera Brown who lightly censured the doggerel. Members of the Guildhall staff, in particular Bob Roberts and Simon Smith of Guildhall Library as well as the Public Relations office and photographer Peter Holland who guided me throughout.

Printed endpaper St. Lawrence Jewry, 1783 by Thomas Malton. Reproduced by courtesy of Guildhall Library.

Graces have been compiled for special occasions over a period of 15 years. During that time personalities who are referred to in them and in the explanatory text, have not infrequently been honoured or have changed their status, or are now deceased. It is hoped that all such references will be regarded as historic and not therefore requiring alterations to the subsequent text. The author apologises to anyone who feels that the problem should have been dealt with otherwise.

Contents

Acknowledgements, v
Contents, vi
List of Illustrations, viii
Forewords, ix, xi
    The First Sea Lord, Admiral Sir Julian Oswald GCB ADC
    Commander and Alderman Sir Robin Gillett Bt, GBE, RD, RNR; Lord Mayor of London 1976-77
Preface, xiii
Profile, xvii

The Livery

The Freedom, 3
Guildhall, 7
The Idea of the Livery, 14
Livery Companies in Order of Precedence, 20
The Shrievalty, 22

Graces on some Livery Company Occasions, 25
    Grocers, 25
    Merchant Taylors, 26
    Haberdashers, 28
    Girdlers, 29
    Fletchers, 32
    Loriners, 39
    Shipwrights, 41
    Spectacle Makers, 59
    Carmen, 63
    Chartered Surveyors, 64
    Chartered Accountants, 68
    Launderers, 69
    Insurers, 78
    Fuellers, 79
    Lightmongers, 80
    Architects, 83
    Constructors, 85

    The City Livery Club, 87

Contents

The Corporation of London

Aldermen and their Wards, 95
The Mayoralty, 100
The Mansion House, 105
    The Dinner Routine, 108
    The Toast List, 112
    Carriages at 1030, 114
Graces on some Committee Occasions, 115
    City Lands & Bridge House Estates, 115
    Coal, Corn & Rates Finance, 118
    Billingsgate, 122
    West Ham Park, 123
    Housing, 123
    General Purposes, 124
    The Police, 124
    The Library, 125
    Establishment, 126
    Spitalfields Market, 126

Graces on Sundry Occasions

Royal Graces, 127
Anniversaries, 129
Celebrations, 134
American Thanksgiving, 135
The Old Bailey, 137
Bovis Centenary, 139
John Coomb: Payne & Gunter's Anniversary, 140
Toastmaster's Graces, 142
Launch of HMS London, 145
Lloyds: Chairman's Dinner, 147
London Tourist Board, 148
New Zealand Waitangi Day, 148
The Ross McWhirter Foundation, 150
Rendel Palmer and Tritton, 154
The Special Constabulary, 154
The Women's National Cancer Control Campaign, 157
The Royal Society of St George, 159
Variety Club of Great Britain, 168

Appendixes, 171
    Greenwich Sermon, 171
    Wednesday Rostrum, 175
Epilogue, 184

List of Illustrations

Grace said from behind the Lord Mayor's chair, xvii

Certificate of Freedom, 4

Guildhall: HM The Queen speaking at the Guildhall Lunch, 8

Terence Cuneo in front of his painting of the Coronation Lunch at Guildhall, 12

The Painted Hall, Greenwich: Trafalgar Night Dinner, 42

Sion College. The City Livery Club, 89

Lord Mayor's Banquet: a reception and presentation in the Old Library, 102

Mansion House, 106

Mansion House Christmas Cards, 107

Banquet in the Egyptian Hall, Mansion House, 109

Laudi Spirituali, 110

'There were Cappadocian Fathers called Basil', 156

The Rt. Hon. J Enoch Powell MBE, 179

Mrs Thatcher. Young Communist demonstrators, 181

Foreword

THE FIRST SEA LORD
ADMIRAL SIR JULIAN OSWALD GCB ADC
SINCE PROMOTED
ADMIRAL OF THE FLEET

It is delightful but daunting to be invited to write a short introduction to *Airs & Graces*. My trepidation is increased by the fact that, in recommending this slim volume to you, the Reader, I am, as it were, providing the initial *Grace* to the sumptuous repast which I know you are about to enjoy. Thus, unwittingly, I find myself competing with the author on his own ground — that of providing the sagacious and witty aperitif for the meal to follow. And I have learned that one should never compete with experts on their own ground! Dear Reader, if you do not already recognise Basil Watson as an expert in pre-prandial pronouncement, you soon will!

The second aspect of my task which gives me pause for thought concerns the Enduring Relationship. I have long recognised that, in many respects and cases, it is the initial relationship between two people which endures. Nowhere is this more true than in the Navy, where we tend to know each other well over a long period. I have frequently heard a senior Admiral address an older and very retired Lieutenant Commander in deferential terms — because the former was, at some stage, the pupil or subordinate of the latter. It is, therefore, not the First Sea Lord who is writing this introduction, but Acting Sub-Lieutenant Julian Oswald, a member of the Reverend Basil Watson's Tutor Set at the Royal Naval College, Greenwich. And what a fine Tutor he was! Exceptionally well and roundly educated himself, with a clear analytical brain, a real sense of history and fine recall, yet always striving to draw out the thoughts and ideas of his pupils rather than imposing his own. To say that we benefited enormously from his help and guidance would be an understatement. We young men, and the Navy as a whole, were more than privileged that Basil gave so many years of his life to our Service.

Foreword

All of us must retire eventually, but the manner of Basil Watson's leaving the Navy is a conundrum to this day. Why he, the obvious and outstanding choice as Chaplain of the Fleet, was denied this office and honour I do not know and cannot understand. But, aghast and disappointed though he must have been, it is a measure of the man that he plunged into the new and totally different milieu of St Lawrence Jewry-next-Guildhall and has played a leading role in religious affairs, and more, in the City as a whole, and many Livery Companies in particular, ever since.

'Home is the sailor, home from the sea . . .' runs the old song. Basil Watson has truly found home in the Square Mile and among its people, and I, for one, am delighted that he has compiled this record. The Navy is not known for heaping too much praise on its people, but we do have one coded group in the signal book meaning 'Very well done'. It seems appropriate to say 'BRAVO ZULU — BASIL WATSON'.

Foreword

COMMANDER AND ALDERMAN
SIR ROBIN GILLETT Bt GBE RD RNR
LORD MAYOR OF LONDON 1976–7

I first met Basil Watson at his interview for the appointment of a new Vicar for the Church of St Lawrence Jewry-next-Guildhall. This is a Guild Church with a mission to the Corporation of London and requiring an incumbent of the highest quality. As a Guild Church, it operates throughout the week but 'never on Sundays' which is the prerogative of the parish churches.

Basil's answer to the interviewing panel chairman's question 'Why do you want to come to St Lawrence Jewry?' was 'Because there is no Mothers' Union and no work on Sundays!' I am sure it clinched his appointment. We like our vicar to have a sense of humour — read this slim volume and you will see what I mean.

This was to be Basil's first 'civil' appointment and the City took him and his wife Jan to their hearts. I served him as one of his Churchwardens throughout his sixteen years in the post.

He on his part served me as my Chaplain when I was Sheriff in 1973–4 and Lord Mayor in 1976–7 and in the matter of Grace saying had his big moment at the lunch in Guildhall after the St Paul's service and walk about on the occasion of Her Majesty The Queen's Silver Jubilee. A worldwide tv/radio audience estimated at 500 million heard his ringing tones as he used George Belling's, ironmonger of Exeter, Grace before the meal.

A big man both physically and spiritually, he transferred his ability to counsel sailors to his new flock of Corporation Staff or worried businessmen. As I said of him in a valedictory speech in Common Council on his retirement, he is 'a Christian who would look the Devil in the eye and the Devil would back-up'.

In addition to serving other Sheriffs and Lord Mayors as Chaplain, he was much in demand by Livery Companies looking for a 'spiritual advisor' and many of the graces contained herein are structured to suit their dinners or installation of their Masters.

Foreword

The 'never on Sunday' phrase may have been true but, for the rest of the week, St Lawrence was a power-house of music, speakers from all walks of life, memorial services, weddings and christenings. He married my younger son, who had been baptised there by the previous incumbent, Frank Trimingham, Chaplain to my Father as Lord Mayor. When Basil married a couple, you felt they really were married and any man trying to 'put them asunder' had better watch out.

It gives me great pleasure to have had my say in this foreword. If, occasionally, an episcopal eyebrow was raised, so what? I am sure a little laughter in Heaven never came amiss.

Preface

Airs & Graces! On one occasion at a Livery Dinner, I was welcomed as an official guest by my witty friend, Peter Grafton. He said I was known as a man of few (h)airs and many graces. His aphorism was well received. I liked it too. It must have been tucked away in my subconscious until it surfaced in its present title form. Both its strands of thought were woven together to give a certain character to my ministry of which this slim volume is an offering. The City has its 'airs'. It has style. Its history, tradition, architecture and accepted ceremonial, expressed with all the pomp and circumstance inextricable from a corporate life, have all merged together with its financial expertise over the centuries to make the City unique. It is those airs which I have tried to identify, especially as I have had the good fortune, in recent years, to be present and there, on a number of the City's formal and celebratory occasions, to say Grace.

Alas, I have lost most of the scraps of paper on which the early graces were written. They were intended in any case to be ephemeral, for that night only. Like the fisherman, as I now look them over at the end of the day, I realise that it must have been the best that got away! Composed in the evening bath before going out to dine, with a glass of scotch at hand, I toyed with ideas in the thought-relaxing leisure of hot water and scribbled them down afterwards. Often they were amended as I walked to one of the many Livery Halls within a few hundred yards of home, St Lawrence Jewry-next-Guildhall, where we lived 'over the shop'. It has been only recently that I have kept my doggerel verses at the suggestion of indulgent Liverymen who thought that they would make amusing reminiscences.

I lived and worked in the City for 16 years. When I retired I went to evening classes with the admirable Lee Waite, the City

Preface

guide-lecturer. He opened my eyes to features of buildings that I had passed in the street hundreds of times but never seen: customs of which I had heard but never comprehended. It is against that City background that I have composed my (dis) Graces. I offer this odd compilation in hope that an insider's view of its corporate life may help to put a little flesh and breathe a personal breath into the dry bones of the Square Mile.

Inevitably, autobiography has crept in: the first person singular. In mitigation, I have to admit to getting my satisfactions in life by taking an immense interest in other people too. 'What did you have?' my wife used to ask me whenever I got home from a dinner. 'I had Bunny Morgan on my right and Jack Neary on my left, and I'll show you the menu card if you really want to know what we had to eat and drink'. And she did, too. In the tranquillity of the following morning, I have recollected and savoured the delicious pleasures of the previous evening's table. In the event, though, my interest has been in people. Over dinner, I have talked endlessly and been a recipient of many confidences. Conversations which began at table have ended on later occasions in the privacy of my vestry and chapel — 'You won't remember me' says the voice on the phone, 'but I sat next to you at dinner three years ago when we talked … can we meet?' On two specific occasions, I have discreetly heard confessions at table and given absolution. It was quite possible to maintain the confidentiality, I may say, when seated, as I often was, at the head of a sprig of the table. Critics have gently chided me for spending more time in a dinner jacket than in my cassock and surplice. I am also conscious that I have done some of my best work so clothed.

Saying Grace posed a problem. Dining two or three times a week in the season, I found no satisfaction, whatever the Almighty derived from it, in saying 'Benedictus benedicat' on every occasion. Besides, I have never since said it without an amused reminder of the first Grace I said at the High Table in the Painted Hall at Greenwich. We were entertaining the Admiral, a Roman Catholic convert, in the Mess that evening. When I sat down after saying the Latin Grace, the Captain of the College, in the Chair, asked why I had not given it in a language that all understood. 'With all due respect, Captain,' chipped in the Admiral, 'that Grace was not given to you but to Someone who understands that language perfectly well'. It was the same Captain who, some time afterwards, was himself President of the first Mess Guest Night after the Queen's accession. I had been chattering to

Preface

Michael Lewis, the Professor of History, my neighbour, when the gavel went. Instinctively, I offered Nelson's Grace as I had on countless occasions. Taken somewhat by surprise, I said 'God save the King . . .' That cost me a round of port in the Painted Hall — a whole month's pay! I have more than recouped the expense, of course, in the number of free Livery Dinners I have enjoyed, but a formal grace, whether in Latin or not, posed another problem for me. It never sounded as though I was doing honour to my hosts or had given thought to the particular occasion. Hence, while theology is always implicit, and most often explicit, it is the secular nature of the proceedings that I have made a means of asking a blessing.

Sometimes, regretfully, the format has offended traditionalists but often enough it has provoked the odd wry smile or the happy laugh which has eased the preliminary tensions of the sitting-down-to-table process, and helped to get the gastric juices working to best advantage. Many, in fact, have been the invitations to dinners 'to get us off to a good start' as my host has said. I've always felt an obligation to do that. I once came home as a teenager from a party that never got going 'dripping like a chief stoker'. My shrewd old mother, a great party girl in her day, gave me the rough side of her tongue and taught me a lesson that I've increasingly valued: 'When you go to a party, see that the party goes'. Working to that precept can be fun. My God has a sense of humour. He can be severe too. He may even take his vengeance on a well-fed face — quite rightly no doubt, from time to time . . . with a bad oyster. What vengeance! Salmonella has, of recent years, proved to be even more devastating. How delicious, though, are the special delights and delicacies, the strawberries and cream of his provision. When they, in fact, have been on the menu, I have often told Lord Denning's story of the diner who amusingly made the waitress understand that he wanted strawberries and — not with — cream. 'You appreciate, dear lady, the difference I'm sure between a woman and child, and a woman with child.'

I have loved it all. I hope the Airs and Graces of my City, as I have been involved in and described them, will be easily digested by all whose memories have been stimulated by them, or who have had their appetites whetted. The fellowship of a City table is a precious bond. The Graces are my personal tribute to its privileged life.

It was while the coffee cups were being cleared away, on a recent occasion at a Fletchers' Company dinner, that a waitress brought me a verse on the back of a menu card. It was from a Liveryman's wife.

Preface

Though written so spontaneously, it says it all and sends me on my ego trip.

> Oh, what a treat! Before we eat
> Here's Basil once more on his feet!
> He bids us all in well-turned phrases
> To thank the Lord and sing His praises;
> And then commends with kindly wit
> Our hosts around whose board we sit.
> Dear Basil, every one's a winner
> By grace, before each City Dinner.
> Ver(a) B(rown)
> Ver(B) (sap)

A banquet in Guildhall with the author between the
Right Honourable The Lord Mayor, Alderman Sir Francis
McWilliams GBE, and the Lady Mayoress, Lady McWilliams,

The Toastmaster, Bernard Sullivan, is at the left of the photograph.

HE GAVELS AND ANNOUNCES

*Pray silence for the Reverend Basil Watson
who will say Grace,*

That sonorous exordium, or something like it, following the three knocks of the toastmaster's gavel, must have been heard reverberating around Mansion House, Guildhall or other historic halls of the Livery Companies of the City of London on several hundred occasions. From early 1970, when I was selected by some 18 members of the General Purposes Committee of the Common Council to be Vicar of its Guild Church, St Lawrence Jewry-next-Guildhall, my life has been caught up in the traditions and colourful routines of the City, of which formal dining occasions are an integral part.

Profile

There were eight of us short-listed for interview from over 100 candidates for the advertised appointment. Taken in alphabetical order, I was the last to appear before the Committee. 'Will you tell us, please' said the Chairman 'why it is that you have applied for the job'. 'If I may use my naval vernacular, Sir, I would say it is because it seemed like money for old rope. I understand that Guild Churches are not allowed to open on Sundays: that there's unlikely to be a Sunday School or a Mothers' Union — what else could a naval chaplain want?'. There were a few belly-laughs but I sensed more lead balloons and heard the Chairman upbraid me for such an answer: 'I'd expected to hear you say that you saw its pastoral opportunities.' However, with three others, I was invited back after lunch. During that time, the Chairman had rung the Lord Mayor's Secretary, Admiral Peter Howes: 'We have a naval chaplain in for this job. Some of the members would like to have him but I think that he has an attitude of levity to the job which doesn't augur too well.' 'If he's a naval chaplain and hasn't got a sense of humour, he'd be no good to you Chairman, or to the City.' Second time round, there were no problems. The Chairman apologised saying that he'd never come across naval humour before: he was delighted to appoint me for five, renewable for three years. In the event, they were good enough to renew my appointment on four further occasions until at 70, like all civic officials, I felt I ought to retire. Sadly!

They were glorious years for which I had been wonderfully prepared by the Navy. It was a job tailor-made for me — God-given, as I understood it — and I wanted nothing else. The Chairman, thinking that I might be tempted away, had emphasised their hope that I would, at least, stay for the five years. He had little idea of the pastoral opportunities that would arise, nor had I: but all sorts of spiritual and human problems arose out of the thousand or so people who sat in our pews each week. It became an enormous workload, carried out perhaps more often in a dinner jacket than in a cassock and surplice. I hope that this collection of Graces captures and conveys some of the warmth of the human relationships that, as the Chaplain, I was able to establish uniquely in the City.

I came to St Lawrence Jewry after 25 years in the Royal Navy which I had joined at the end of 1943 — not till then, as Chaplains were required to have five years' professional training before joining up. After a further year in Cambridge as a curate (at Holy Trinity),

Profile

I went to a pit parish in Northumberland, inspired by the Bevin Boys to do so. It was a complete culture shock as it was an area which had known the full force of those terrible years of unemployment just over the river from Jarrow. I was to bury some teenagers who died of TB contracted through malnutrition in the days of the Means Test. I experienced the conditions — then improving — on which the academic Marxists of the Cambridge History School of my time (I was a contemporary of Burgess & Maclean) indicted the class struggle provoked by Capitalism. That never seemed to worry the magnificent Geordies whose dialect I was always to detect later on, making me feel instantly at home wherever we were.

I was at sea within a very short time of leaving my parish. There were 700 of us in that first ship: an American-built Escort Carrier, HMS *Attacker*. From January '44 till end of '45, we operated in the Atlantic as part of a diversionary force on D-Day, going on to give air cover in the Mediterranean, especially to the South of France landings. We were involved in the Italian campaign and, more extensively, in the liberation of Greece and the Greek Islands, operating out of Alexandria. We went on to take part in the Japanese war after an extensive refit at Taranto.

The transit of the Suez Canal gave me the chance to cable at one end of it and get a reply at the other, a proposal of marriage to Janibel. It was all done by coded numbers which the GPO turned into a romantic telegram at the receiving end. It was, in fact, telephoned to Lake House, the Orthopaedic Hospital for the Airborne Division where Jan was senior physiotherapist to Colonel Charnley — later to be Sir John for his pioneering work on hip replacement surgery. 'Answer the phone please, Miss Roderick' said the Matron in the midst of doctor's rounds — 'anything important?'. 'Nothing, Matron: just one for me'. Janibel, the daughter of a well-known academic doctor in Cambridge was a front-row high-kicker in Prunella Stack's Health and Beauty. We'd met in my last months in Cambridge when, alas, I was already committed to the slums of Newcastle. My pursuit cooled when I realised that it was not the place for the likes of her, or so I thought. However, our desultory correspondence sparked into life when we met before I sailed and that 6-week long refit at Taranto gave us the chance of a regular mail . . . we were married, to live happily ever after, a fortnight after I got home after VJ-Day. Our son, Roderick and daughter, Clarissa, now of course grown-up and established, give us great joy.

Profile

Engagement gave an added dimension to my life! I needed it too in the attempt to keep up morale in the ship. After VE-Day, the further Japanese war was not faced with enthusiasm: the ship was not built for the tropics: the enemy was well-entrenched in Malaya: we were rated 'expendable'. I can still feel the surge of relaxed tension as I stepped out of the caboose where, as ship's broadcaster, I had announced the dropping of the A-Bomb. Little did I know what it meant except to venture, with more assurance, that phrase which kept us going: 'home for Christmas'. I have never had much time for the armchair moralists who deplore Hiroshima and Nagasaki. Like the late Group Captain Lord Leonard Cheshire, VC, as we've all known that great saint of a man, I've regretted not the use but the method of the bomb's delivery. Critics have little idea of the prevailing stress among our gathering fleets and armies and good morality is, in large part, the achieving of the possible. There was little doubt in my mind of the job we had to finish — and to do so quickly.

Demobilisation — Selwyn College invited me back as Chaplain. I'd been scholarly lazy, as an undergraduate, though I'd been a College prizeman and been awarded a pre-war post graduate scholarship to Tübingen in Germany. I'd also been President of Athletics and played rugger and hockey in the Cuppers: nothing wonderful but adequate for membership of Hawks. However, I no longer felt attracted to academia after being where the action was. Nor did I see myself as a curate in suburbia. When pressure was put on me to stay in the Navy, I felt that it was my scene: as did Janibel. Even when we had experienced periods of separation and I was offered the prestigious job of St Stephen's, Rochester Row, to follow George Reindorp (later Bishop of Guildford and of Salisbury), we still felt, both of us, that the Navy offered us greater realism and immediacy with people and, for me, a chance of still being a priest without being, so to speak, a clergyman. Until, much later, when I got to know the City clergy, I fear that I had the average layman's attitude to 'the cloth'.

I had been ordained largely as a result of the Bryan Green Mission to Cambridge. Having read history for my degree, I switched to theology and went on to Westcott House where I became Head Boy (Sheriff) in the great days of 'BK' Cunningham. 'More heart, less head' was BK's helpful stricture and, as the only rule of the House was 'No smoking cigars in chapel', we were left to make our own rules of life. They were wonderful growing, ripening days. Bryan Green continued as a strong influence and came to Culdrose for me when I was serving

Profile

with the Fleet Air Arm (1950–52) to conduct a week's Mission. On his arrival, Lieutenant Ray Lygo (now Admiral Sir Raymond and lately Chief Executive of British Aerospace) flew his squadron past in the formation of a cross *in hoc signo vinces*. Admiral Sir Donald Gibson, in his autobiography, records the influence of the Mission on him (and I prepared him for confirmation) and, over the years, many a sailor has

> JUST REMEMBER BRYAN. THE VALLEY OF THE SHADOW OF DEATH IS NOTHING COMPARED TO A CHIEF'S MESS AT TOT TIME.

spoken to me about it. Bryan Green was later kind enough to suggest that I should follow Pat Gilliat at Holy Trinity, Brompton (before its recent 'born-again' repute) but, by then, the influence of my Woodard School (Worksop) had firmly come through and asserted itself in making me the Prayer Book Catholic–1662 Establishment man, that I am. Holy Trinity Brompton was well declined for St Lawrence Jewry.

From 1952–5, I had the great good fortune to be Chaplain at the Royal Naval College, Greenwich. There were two of us academically qualified to be appointed to the civilian teaching staff: honours degrees in History or English were essential. There were 300 students, and chaplains could only be borne on a capitation basis of 600: so we wore the two hats half time. Among other distinguished sub-lieutenants in my particular tutor set was the present First Sea Lord, Admiral Sir Julian Oswald, and, of Falklands fame, Admiral Sir Sandy Woodward. Additionally, I was entrusted with the complete restoration and liturgical reorganisation of the world-famous Chapel after its wartime neglect and bomb blast damage. I was left there for three years to see that work through to its reconsecration by the Archbishop of Canterbury (Dr Fisher) in the presence of the Queen Mother. David

Profile

(now Lord) Eccles was then Minister of Works and, good Churchman that he is, aided and abetted to an enormous sum of money the work I proposed to his Ancient Monuments department: and to so many of the artists and craftsmen of the period. It was a time of privileged, enriching cultural growth. The College put me up for my OBE and, most appreciatively, made me a Life Honorary Member of the Mess. This is something which Janibel and I frequently have pleasure in exercising as we now, in retirement, live just outside its West Gate (a 1989 sermon appears in the Appendix)

For three months after its completion, I had the thrill of conducting worship in all its grandeur with congregations filling even the galleries. We organised a Thames launch to run from Westminster in time for church, with lunch afterwards in the National Maritime Museum. I loved that fulfilment of a vision of things 'being decently done and in order'. I was then drafted to Malta but what I lost in splendour I found in the unique character of submariners who allowed me to go day running in 'the boats' most weeks and to celebrate Holy Communion in the fore-ends. I was not treated as a descendant of Jonah. Getting to know their great wartime heroes like Tony Miers VC, Godfrey Place VC and Ben Bennington DSO and three bars, was another great bonus to the appointment to the First Submarine Squadron.

Malta also gave us the chance of being together as a family, established at Marsa Scala with a mooring just outside the back door and everything that turned the kids into water babies and more. They attended the Dockyard School at Verdala as did the children of the then Prime Minister, Dom Mintoff. Our wives, who had both nursed in Oxford, met 'collecting the children'. As he and I turned out to be within ten days for age, a family friendship was formed which, with a week as their guests last year, continues to this day. We played tennis at their home and swam at Cyclops quite frequently. It was at the time of the break-up of the Empire generally and of Malta's problem of integration/independence in particular. I think I knew Dom's mind on this and on the changed thinking on defence requirements. The Governor, General Sir Robert Laycock (Evelyn Waugh's *Officers and Gentlemen*), knew of our discreet friendship and frequently invited us to San Anton. When the Senior Chaplain tried to send me home for unpatriotic disloyalty, the Governor intervened to keep me as a valuable interpreter of what he called 'the bellyaches'. I also had a fascinating ecclesiastical commission from Dom Mintoff to call on the Cardinal Archbishop of Venice, whom he regarded as an urbane

Profile

(ex-Papal Nuncio in Paris) and liberal churchman. My role was to explain the nature of the church problem in Malta and to assure him that were Dom Mintoff in London he would be a regular attender at Farm Street, but he could not, with the cultivated brain of the Rhodes Scholar, accept the medieval superstitions of a Church untouched by the counter-Reformation. I had a fascinating hour with the Archbishop and, thereafter, a very different attitude to the Throne of St Peter, for he was, some six months after, to be elected Pope John XXIII.

We came home to an appointment in Portsmouth — HMS *Vernon* which was very accessible from Chichester where we were lucky enough to be able to rent a house in the Close. I found myself doing a lot of Cathedral and public school preaching and being invited by the BBC to broadcast and, on several occasions, do the TV Epilogue. I believe that these activities were responsible for my being invited by Dick Janvrin (now Vice Admiral Sir Richard) to be his Chaplain when he took command of the great Fleet Carrier HMS *Victorious*. He nursed the Drake ideal of a united ship: 'all of one company'. Carriers could be notoriously divided, especially with a crew of 2500, half of whom worked on the upper deck, the rest below, driving and provisioning the ship: in sailors' language 'waafoos and fish-heads'. 'I will have the gentlemen to haul and draw with the mariners and the mariners with the gentlemen'. With that in mind, he invited me to take over the broadcasting and to produce a newspaper, both ship-uniting activities. Each night at Pipedown, I spoke for ten minutes or so trying to knit together the events of the day — lots of gossip, in what we called Round Up. Then, overnight, we produced a newspaper, VicNews, notable for promoting TUGG, who was to become the Navy's own cartoonist. I tried to reproduce John Freeman-type programmes — 'face-to-face' — with any of the VIPs who visited for one reason or another. Among them was Flag Officer, Far East, Admiral Sir Michael le Fanu. We did three broadcasts while he flew his flag in Victorious: there were no holds barred and we discussed everything from our presence East of Suez to his marriage to a wife who was then so paralysed that he physically carried her wherever they went, not least around the dance floor. He was one of the Navy's great characters who did me the honour later, when he heard of my premature retirement from the Navy, of asking me to reconsider my decision as he had hoped that, if he became First Sea Lord, he would have me as his Chaplain of the Fleet.

Profile

I bargained my radio and press activity with the Captain for the restoration of 'compulsory church' on Sunday mornings. We called it General Assembly so as not to contravene regulations. A thousand of us at church on the flight deck, lustily encouraged to sing by the Royal Marines Band, has been unforgettable by many of that commission.

.... AND AFTER THAT BIT ABOUT *YOU* SINGIN' HYMNS ON THE FLIGHT DECK, I DIDN'T BELIEVE ANOTHER WORD YOU WROTE.

'It's good to be back at church, padre' said a CPO, 'we all feel we can come now that it's compulsory'. It was, of course, the ultimate expression of our unity, fulfilling that larger purpose explicit in what used to be the First Article of War when I joined the Navy — 'the worship of Almighty God'. For me, that commission was the crowning of my naval career.

It was a punishing routine that I worked but stood me in great stead when I went to the States. I was invited by the English Speaking Union to be one of 20 whom they sent to cover the States: preaching, speaking at Rotary lunches, giving endless interviews to the press. On one of the Sundays in August, I preached in the National Presbyterian Church — 'Eisenhower's Church' — in Nebraska Avenue, Washington. There was a huge congregation and, in the glad-handing afterwards, I was asked for a copy of my sermon by someone who said he would get it printed in the Record. When I told my host, he encouraged me to forgo the afternoon's tennis/bathing party and write out what I had said from my notes. 'It is not many Americans who have their

Profile

sermons printed in the Congressional Record: it must be unique for an Englishman.' Senator Stennis, senator responsible for the Armed Forces, was as good as his word.

Proceedings of the 90th Congress: Second Session, Vol. 114, No. 164
'Mr Stennis: Mr President, recently it was my privilege to hear an outstanding and challenging sermon delivered at the National Presbyterian Church in Washington by the Revd. Basil Watson, a visiting minister from London, England. Revd. Watson is a member of the British Navy and the Chaplain of the Royal Naval College in London. The sermon reflects the fine character and spiritual strength of Revd. Watson and shows also a broad understanding of the practical problems that face us, not only in England but also in America and elsewhere. I ask unanimous consent to have the Sermon printed in the Record.'
So it was.

I was fortunate to be invited back to the States each August for twenty years. Last year, I did a farewell round, staying a night or two with each of the seven couples I'd married over the years from Seattle to San Diego. I was a great West Coast man. My American exposure enriched my Ministry greatly and loosened me up in every way for the wonderfully varied life I was to have in the City.

The Wednesday Rostrum, with its speakers covering such a spectrum of interests, will probably be associated with my time and concept of the role of a Guild church. A rationale of that activity and the list of the distinguished contributors to the ordeal, appears as an Appendix. I was able to make the acquaintance of many of them when they were guests at City or Livery dinners. While others were entering, I was detained to go in procession with the VIPs so as to slot into position behind the chair (symbolically the Chaplain is the voice of the host). On that personal contact, I was later able to capitalise and achieve that remarkable list of speakers. The Graces, in that way, cover a number of years in the political life of the nation and of the financial personalities of the City. They belong to the era when socialising was a natural part of doing business, eyeball to eyeball; when everyone knew the strengths and weaknesses of those who tried to uphold the moral status of the City. I was glad that I went into retirement with Big Bang. I am, though, equally grateful to my successor who warmly welcomes me back for duties with families in whose lives I became so pastorally involved during my incumbency.

Profile

Over the years, I became Chaplain to the Lord Mayor, Sir Robin Gillett, and to some six of the Sheriffs. That gave me the thrill of travelling the route of the Lord Mayor's Show in the Gold and other coaches, as well as eating my way through those special Banquets. At various times, I was, either as Company or Master's, chaplain to 19 Livery companies. I tried to show my interest in all of them by composing a personalised Grace, albeit often in the excruciating doggerel to which this collection bears witness. I was invited to most of the Corporation's Committee dinners and to the annual banquets of six national organisations. What I probably enjoyed most was being involved, as I still am, in so many families' occasions from baptisms to golden weddings; and in those fascinating round table conversations at partners' lunches when the moral issues of the day were discussed. Theology too, perhaps surprisingly, was often at issue.

Though it was re-built after the war, St Lawrence Jewry was unmistakably Wren, with whom, of course, I had a long 'acquaintance' at Greenwich. Fortunately, its distinguished architect Cecil Brown was still active and I used to enjoy it when he dropped in each month just to be at home in his own creation. He had also designed, within its framework, unseen to the unknowing, a vicarage of exceptional merit in which we delighted to live and entertain. Our roof garden — skips of best topsoil provided by courtesy of Trollope & Colls (Vic (Lord) Matthews) in lieu of oversailing rent, while their tower crane worked on the West Wing of Guildhall — became a Derry & Toms feature. By way of thanking him for all that, I was able to raise sufficient funds to complete that part of the fabric which he had not been able to finish originally. He delighted in the wrought-iron screen which the Royal Marines provided to mark their affiliation to St Lawrence Jewry as their London church. Strangely, we nearly fell out over it! 'You can't ask them to do that work — far too crude for my church'. He didn't know the Royals as I did. He was his gracious self again when their centrepiece was put in place: 'do you think you could ask them to do the two additional gates as well?'

In the event, with the necessary RM template, the Airborne and the Parachute Regiments, thanks to General Sir Anthony Farrar Hockley, completed this arresting and delicate feature of the church. I loved the feel of the church: prayers and thoughts mellowed as one moved around in it: music so gloriously too, organ and piano, ministering to the soul. City workers loved it. There was hardly a moment in the day

Profile

when someone was not sitting quietly in a pew. There were those who dropped in on their way to work, to give a sense of purpose to their daily round; and those who wrestled with weighty matters: 'I've been here for two hours struggling' said a well-known tycoon, 'I want to thank God that the sheer beauty of the place, and what it stands for, has put my problem in perspective'. I was there to lend an ear to the over-stressed and to hear burdened confessions. How privileged! I hope that the Church of England will continue to be the church with a ministry to all our fellow-citizens and to provide an Order in which priests can experience the joyful satisfaction of their calling.

The Corporation did me the signal honour of an exceptional Resolution in Common Council on my retirement: 'to record members' great appreciation of his devoted service over 16 years — throughout this time he has given the Corporation, the Livery and many others, the benefit of his guidance in matters spiritual. The candid, indeed forthright, expression of orthodox Christian views has been appreciated throughout the City — he has, by stimulating interest in those working and living in the City, contributed greatly to the involvement of the Church with its community, etc. etc.'

I trust that, like my selecting Chairman, an attitude of levity — godly levity? — will still be detected in what *Airs & Graces* has to offer. I also hope that the voice in which grace is said will carry with it not just the stentorian tones of the quarterdeck trained in gale force winds, but some of the timbre that has emerged from a fascinating and most enjoyable life. In profile, at any rate, that is how I see Basil Watson who says grace.

The Livery

The Freedom

Anyone wishing to become a liveryman and take part in the corporate life of the City must become a Freeman. That will occasion a visit to Guildhall where, in the Court of the Chamberlain, a simple but awesome ceremony takes place. It involves making a declaration.

The Declaration of a Freeman

> I do solemnly declare that I will be good and true to our Sovereign Lady Queen Elizabeth II; that I will be obedient to the Mayor of this City; that I will maintain the Franchises and Customs thereof, and will keep this City harmless, in that which in me is; that I will also keep the Queen's Peace in my own person; that I will know no Gatherings nor Conspiracies made against the Queen's Peace, but I will warn the Mayor thereof, or hinder it to my power; and that all these points and articles I will well and truly keep, according to the Law and Customs of this City, to my power.

The Declaration is then signed and a parchment certificate (a copy of Freedom) given. An invitation almost invariably follows to an adjacent hospitality room where, in a glass of madeira, a toast is proposed to 'the youngest Freeman'. There is a modest fee to pay which goes entirely towards maintaining the City of London Freeman's School in Ashtead, Surrey.

The Freedom is available to all British or Commonwealth citizens of good character, male or female, above the age of twenty-one. Naturalised British citizens are equally eligible. There is no question of having to be born within the sound of Bow Bells, or reside within the Square Mile. The Freedom is there for the asking and the Corporation particularly appreciates those who take it up wishing to further the spirit of its traditions. Ulterior motives for doing so are almost totally ruled out, as its tangible benefits are limited to certain

Certificate of Freedom.

London] Basil Aldersons Watson, O.B.E., Citizen and Haberdasher of London was admitted
To Wit.] into the Freedom aforesaid and made the Declaration required by Law in the Mayoralty of
Sir Ian Frank Bowater, G.B.E., D.S.O., T.D., Mayor and Charles Richard Whittington, Esquire, M.C.
Chamberlain and is entered in the Book signed with the Letter D 3 relating to the Purchasing of
Freedoms and the Admissions of Freemen (to wit) the 24th day of July in the 19th Year of
the reign of Queen Elizabeth II And in the Year of our Lord 1970. In Witness whereof the Seal of the
Office of Chamberlain of the said City is hereunto affixed Dated in the Chamber of the Guildhall of
the same City the day and Year aforesaid.

The Freedom

educational advantages and charitable alms-housing for the sick and needy.

The Freedom was, dating from some 700 years ago, essential for those who wished to trade in the City. As the trades, guilds or what are now our Livery Companies emerged in the Middle Ages, they set themselves certain standards of skill and acceptable behaviour. They controlled employment, apprenticed the young and cared for the elderly and sick. Their members, however, had to have additional permission — the Freedom — to work in the City.

That requirement prevailed until 1856 when the Corporation passed legislation, acknowledging the vast expansion of trading, which abolished discrimination against those who did not hold the passport of Freedom. Trading rights and privileges had been substantial though the Freedom had not, alas, conveyed the colourful myths and legends of the right to drive sheep over London bridge or be hanged by a silken cord!

For the most part, the Freedom is taken up by would-be Liverymen who achieve the traditional voting status in Common Hall by doing so. There are three recognised categories:

1 Patrimony. Freedom by patrimony is for children born in lawful wedlock to a Freeman. It was in this way that Prince Charles, through the Fishmongers, took his Freedom in 1971.

2 Servitude. Freedom by service as an apprentice — bound to a tradesman — for four to seven years, between the ages of 14–21. Livery companies still bind apprentices.

3 Redemption. Freedom by purchase. The once high fees, when the Freedom conveyed substantial trading advantages, as well as giving exemption from road, bridge and market tolls, have been reduced to a nominal charge that does little more than cover costs.

I was singularly honoured by the Spectacle Makers (q.v.) by the rare grant of Freedom/Livery by presentation.

Altogether different is the Honorary Freedom. It is the highest honour the Corporation can confer, and it is the same Freedom, but in this case it is awarded and cannot be claimed. Recipients are usually the members of the Royal Family: British and Commonwealth Prime Ministers who have given approximately ten years' service in the office: and wartime leaders of our Fleets and Armies. Several of their statues and memorials adorn Guildhall.

The Order Paper for meetings of Common Council usually includes many names, from all walks of life, whose request for Freedom has to

The Freedom

be approved by the Court. Their willingness to undertake the obligations of Freedom demonstrates the continuing high regard for the City and, in particular, shows an appreciation for its unique governing body, and the vital role it plays in regulating the conditions in which the business City operates.

There is an active Guild of Freemen.

Guildhall

Guildhall was the hall of the Guilds, as the various trades of medieval England were called. It was the repository of the standards and secrets of the Freemen/Liverymen of those crafts and skills.

It is usually dated at 1411, the work of William Croxton. Over the centuries, there were additions to it both in length and height, the most notable addition being the front porch in 1789 by George Dance, the younger, whose father built the Mansion House. When it was restored after WW2, the old hammer-beamed ceiling was replaced by fibre glass, of eye-deceiving quality. There is still evidence of its original role in City life, for example, in the brass lengths let into the stone floor as the definitive standards of measurement. All tradesmen who wished to work in the City, to be Free of it, had to conform to its regulatory discipline. It is, today, the home of the Guilds' successors, the Livery Companies. It is the focus of the corporate life of the City, within the framework of the nation's history.

Starting at the bottom of the west window, in the left-hand corner, is the Coat of Arms of King John. This and the crests of all subsequent Monarchs appear in coloured glass, spaced by the leaded chevrons containing the name of the Lord Mayor for each year of the reign. It was King John who, in the same year as Magna Carta, 1215, granted the citizens of London the right to elect a mayor each year. He was the only person present at Runnymede who was not a Baron. His election takes place in Guildhall on Michaelmas Day, the citizens of London being its Liverymen. The first mayor so recorded is Henry FitzAlwyn in 1189.

In the east window is Richard Whittington, three times elected (Lord) Mayor of London 1397–8: 1406–7: 1419–20.

Fixed to the ceiling are the heraldic shields of all the Livery Companies, beginning with the Mercers' Company whose charter dates from 1347; though the oldest, the Weavers, probably dates from 1184. Jutting out from the walls are the flags of the Great Twelve Companies, so called because of their accumulated wealth through incorporation from the Medieval period, and their consequent power.

Guildhall

Guildhall: HM The Queen speaking at the Guildhall lunch to mark the 40th anniversary of her Accession (her 'Annus horribilis' speech).
Photograph by courtesy of Philip D. Dorell.

The Seniority of the Great Twelve

>Mercers
>Grocers
>Drapers
>Fishmongers

Guildhall

> Goldsmiths
> Skinners
> Merchant Taylors
> Haberdashers
> Salters
> Ironmongers
> Vintners
> Clothworkers

The mnemonic taught me by that most knowledgeable and amusing of City guide-lecturers, Mr Lee Waite, as a means of remembering their seniority reads: 'My God, Do For Goodness Sake Make Haste Since I'm Very Cold'. From the ordering of the Companies in seniority comes, for example, the expression that, when things are in confusion, they are set at sixes and sevens. Both the Merchant Taylors and the Skinners received their Charters on the same day. Seniority was determined by a ruling in 1484 of the Lord Mayor — Billesden — that each would take it for the year in turn to be sixth.

In the gallery, at either end, are the massive figures of Gog and Magog, the mythical giants who stand guard over the City's corporate life. It was natural that it should have been the wish of Sir Winston Churchill, after they had been damaged in the fire raid on the City on 30 December 1940, that they should be speedily replaced. In their present form, they were restored in 1953, the gift of Alderman Sir George Wilkinson (Lord Mayor 1940–41). The figures were carved in limewood by David Evans. They stand 9 feet 3 inches in height, Gog to the North and Magog to the South. Their predecessors had stood in Guildhall since 1708. Previously, they were mobile being paraded in the summer pageants during the 15th and 16th centuries.

Legend has it that they represent the ancient inhabitants of Britain who resisted the invasion of the Trojans some thousand years before the Christian era. Shakespeare had known them as Gogmagog and Corineus. Londoners found that too much of a mouthful and renamed them Gog and Magog.

At ground level, particularly along the north wall, are monuments to our national heroes. In an alcove nearest to the west door is Oscar Nemon's statue of Sir Winston — seated in defiant bulldog pose. Lord Moran records how agreeable to Winston was the prospect of his statue being beneath those of Gog and Magog and alongside Nelson and Wellington with Pitt and Chatham.

Guildhall

Such are some of the evidences of the continuity of our nation's history and its rich tapestry of events, personalities and emblems woven together and finding their expression in this living building. It is in this setting that diners have the good fortune to be entertained on significant occasions, not least at the Annual Lord Mayor's Banquet, on the Monday following the Lord Mayor's Show. It is then that the Prime Minister makes a speech on the state of the nation. This is a magnificent televised occasion. The Archbishop, The Lord Chancellor and leading representatives of all aspects of national life are there. Only when Royalty is present is the top table placed on the dais. On all other occasions, it is arranged in front of the south wall with the presiding chair of the Lord Mayor under the civic canopy, which has rests for the City Sword and Mace. On the occasion that I was Chaplain to Commander Sir Robin Gillett, after a long fanfare of trumpets, I said a Grace of contrasting naval brevity, attributed to Nelson, to feature Sir Robin's years at sea: 'God save The Queen: Bless our victuals and make us thankful, Amen.'

A royal occasion in Guildhall

The Queen's Silver Jubilee on 7 June 1977 must still be, for many, an unique memory. After attending a Service of Thanksgiving in St Paul's Cathedral, HM The Queen went 'walk about' in Cheapside and through King Street into the Guildhall. There, the Lord Mayor, Commander Sir Robin Gillett Bt, GBE, RD, RNR, DSc, with the Lady Mayoress, hosted a luncheon in Her Majesty's honour.

As only on Royal occasions, the top table was arranged on the dais. In the sconces of the ornate carved wooden screen which surrounds it, the City's gold plate was displayed: suffused by concealed lighting, it was a glistening background to the gathering.

Seating plan at the Top Table
Captain Mark Phillips, CVO, ADC
The Duke of Beaufort KG, GCVO
Her Excellency Mrs Kaunda
The Rt Hon James Callaghan, MP
HRH The Prince Andrew
Mrs Coggan
His Beatitude the President of the Republic of Cyprus
HRH The Princess Anne, Mrs Mark Phillips GCVO

Guildhall

King Constantine II of Bogota
HM Queen Elizabeth, the Queen Mother
The Rt Hon The Lord Mayor
HM The Queen
HRH The Prince Philip, Duke of Edinburgh, KG, KT, OM, GBE
The Lady Mayoress
HRH The Prince of Wales, KG, KT, GCB
The Most Reverend and Rt Hon The Lord Archbishop of Canterbury
HRH The Princess Margaret, Countess of Snowdon, CI, GCVO
Admiral of the Fleet, Earl Mountbatten of Burma, KG, GCB, OM, GCSI, GCIE, GCVO, DSO, ADC
Mrs Callaghan
HRH The Prince Edward
The Duchess of Beaufort
His Excellency the President of the Republic of Zambia

To entertain his Monarch in this fashion was, of course, the special day in his Mayoralty for Sir Robin Gillett. Something of what he must have been feeling was expressed in his speech, made when proposing the Loyal Toast.

> 'MAY IT PLEASE YOUR MAJESTY.
> 'In my office in the Mansion House stands a photograph which has accompanied me in many appointments both afloat and ashore.
> 'It shows your dear father inspecting the Cadets at the Nautical College, Pangbourne, on Founder's Day, 4 June 1943. With him, because your mother was unwell, is Your Majesty, aged 17 years 2 months. The Cadet Officer as right marker of the rear rank is me, aged 17 years, 7 months.
> 'Never did I dream that, 34 years later, almost to the day, I would carry the sword of my City before my Sovereign in the House of my God at that girl's Silver Jubilee Thanksgiving Service. And so it is with particular pride and satisfaction that I claim the right of this ancient office to try, sincerely, if inadequately, to express the thanks of the City and the Nation for the first 25 years of Your Majesty's reign.'

There followed a fascinating summary of those 25 years, expressing

Terence Cuneo in front of his painting of the Coronation lunch at Guildhall.
Photograph by courtesy of Universal Pictorial Press.

the warmth of affection in which the Queen was held. He concluded with civic pride.

> 'May I, on behalf of all your subjects, give the Toast on everyone's lips today — "Her Majesty the Queen" '

Thus was set the seal on a day when the City lived to its motto: *Domine Dirige Nos*.

Guildhall

As Lord Mayor's Chaplain, I had the privilege of saying Grace on this occasion from behind the Royal Chair:

GRACE
God bless our meat
God guide our ways
God give us grace
His name to praise
And ever keep in health serene
Elizabeth our gracious Queen.

The occasion was televised and requests from home and abroad came for copies of the Grace.

It was my adaptation of a grace by George Belling, an ironmonger of Exeter, who composed it in 1565 in the reign of Elizabeth I. As it appears in the Harp Book of Graces, edited by John Trench, it reads:

God bless our meat
God guide our waies
God give us grace
Our Lord to please
Lord long preserve in peace and health
Our gracious Queen Elizabeth

The Idea of The Livery

If wining and dining in the best places is all that the Livery means, I would have had my fill long ago. I would certainly not have tried, over the years, to have put my thoughts about the Livery into Graces reflecting the life and activity as well as the personalities involved in its various Companies. Not that I do not enjoy the fleshpots — I do — not half! Especially so in retirement when one lives on shorter, less exotic commons as a rule. Fortunately, I have had my own prescription for girth control which has worked well. In weight, I remain constant.

How good are the best places. Each of the 39 Livery Halls is an expression of character, sometimes in terms of architecture, more frequently, of decoration. In them, on display, are the colourful arms, illuminated Charters and Ordinances; banners; paintings of past Masters and many beautiful pieces of furniture and silver, bequests usually, over the centuries, of wealthy liverymen. From the Jacobean panelling of the Apothecaries' Hall to the exquisite plaster ceiling of the modern Plaisterers', and to the country house atmosphere of the Girdlers standing as it does in its own prize-winning garden in EC2, each Hall conveys its uniqueness and varied associations. What better ambience could there be for social occasions? Companies are not exclusive about the use of their Halls and frequently allow many other Liveries, not so fortunate as to have their own, to use them; as well as organisations involved in charitable activities. What distinctive character they give as well to receptions after the daughters of Liverymen have been married in one of the nearby 33 City churches.

Wine cellars are, for their content, sights to behold. All companies have their wine committees of long experienced amateur tasters, fortified by the merchants and Masters of Wine. As a drinker, usually of average plonk at home, I savour with enormous pleasure the fine wines laid down in vintage years. 'Wine that maketh glad the heart of man'. So too with food.

What a difference has been made to the menus by the advent of the young ladies! Pru Leith, Jean Alexander and others started catering in a small way at partners' lunch tables in City firms, and moved on to

The Idea of The Livery

challenge the monopolies of the established catering companies. After John Coomb had finished his long association with Ring and Brymer, he also brought the highest standards of waitress service to these occasions through his firm, Payne and Gunter. Silently, speedily and without interrupting conversation, courses are served and plates spirited away almost by stealth. Wine waiters are never absent. All takes place within a formalised routine and to meet strict timing requirements: 'Carriages at 10.30pm.' The social columns of the quality press may well record the occasion on the following day. Those notices, to the uninitiated, may seem to be unrelated to contemporary society though all companies that have been granted letters patent since WW2, bear the name of their professional institute as in the Chartered Surveyors and the Chartered Accountants. Outsiders will certainly be unaware of all that lies behind the pleasures of enjoying such good food and wine in the friendships fostered by the traditions and customs of the Livery. What does that amount to in practice? What, in fact, is the idea of the Livery?

Civic pride
Most importantly it implies civic pride, a sense of civic responsibility. Visibly, Liverymen are seen exercising that role in Guildhall on Midsummer Day and at Michaelmas. On the former occasion, they throng the place in an assembly, called Common Hall, to elect the Sheriffs for the year: and then, at Michaelmas, to nominate the candidates for the Mayoralty from whom the Aldermen will make the final choice. Whereas, everywhere else in the country, they are appointed — 'pricked' — by the Monarch since the 12th century, the City has had this unique privilege of choosing its own Sheriffs. Monarchs knew that Liverymen were men of substance whose judgements could be trusted and whose self-interest in their trade meant that they would act with civic responsibility. They had also, of course, especially pledged their allegiance to the Monarch and vowed obedience to the Mayor 'to maintain the franchises and customs thereof and to keep this City harmless in that which in me is'. It is a good sight on these occasions to see Liverymen being checked by the Beadle at the Company wicket-gate into Guildhall and to hear the Serjeant-At-Arms proclaim at the beginning of the proceedings that, on pain of imprisonment, none but Liverymen are to be present. These elective rights are, nowadays, more formal than valuable, but they are a reminder that an historic privilege conveys a continuing responsibility. A sense

The Idea of The Livery

of civic responsibility is a mark of a Liveryman: he is conscious of being a citizen of no mean city.

The pursuit of excellence
A Liveryman has pride in the pursuit of excellence: that is the hallmark of his work. Literally so at Goldsmiths' Hall where the Assay Office is still located and the coin of the Realm is annually tested at the 'trial of the pyx'. All gold and silver and platinum articles are marked and guaranteed genuine. Metaphorically too this is the ideal. From their inception, the Livery Companies, through their Charters and Ordinances, imposed, through their Court of Assistants, quality control on their craft or trade (the 'Baker's Dozen' was self-defensive against a possible charge of giving underweight) and regulated the training of apprentices and supervision of journeymen. Fishmongers appointed, and still do, inspectors of all fish coming in to Billingsgate, and Gun makers 'prove' hand guns and mark them lock stock and barrel. Livery status was granted only to those who were well and truly qualified. This has been a principle of insistence in the formation of the post-war Companies. Only professionals, those properly qualified in their trade and business, can be admitted to that Livery. Through the exercise of patrimony, no doubt the particular professional requirement of membership will be diluted, but, at this stage of development, it is the standard of achievement that is upheld. At a time in national life when work is chosen and rewards are measured almost exclusively in terms of money, it is a salutary corrective to have a body of people who ideally approach their work with respect for the integrity of whatever the vocation may be, and who see it as a means of the service they can give to the community. The pursuit of excellence is the ideal.

The practice of benevolence
Benevolence is an attitude to life which is not, of course, exclusive to the Livery, but it is essential to any understanding of it. Indeed, so much is it at the heart of the Livery ideal that every new Company seeking recognition from the Court of Aldermen must first establish a Charitable Fund of £100,000. Companies, after all, started as self help associations of like-minded craft and tradesmen, and contributed, at the end of the day, towards meeting the major expense, then as now, of funerals. (Some companies have preserved their funeral palls.) With the increase in prosperity and the accumulation of capital,

The Idea of The Livery

the Companies enlarged their benevolence to all sections of the community. They are today always generous subscribers to national and civic good causes, and to as many charities as Liverymen have interests. Almshouses, with care for the sick and senior citizens, are a notable feature. Education even more so. University scholarships, research studentships, professorial chairs, are as much a feature of today's endowments as were school foundations and bursaries of old.

Many a Liveryman's son has been educated at schools founded by his Company:

Mercers:	St Pauls
Grocers:	Oundle
Drapers:	Bancrofts
Skinners:	Tonbridge
Merchant Taylors:	Merchant Taylors
Haberdashers:	Askes
Brewers:	Aldenham

Companies can give a most human and exciting account of the stewardship of their wealth, and can justify their financial privilege to the last penny.

The defence of the Realm
A patriotic sense of duty through the Services is very much a feature of the Livery. Several Liverymen working in London are members of the Honourable Artillery Company based in Armoury House in City Road. They do additional duty in the Company of Pikemen and Musketeers. In Tudor rig, carrying historic arms, they are often seen on ceremonial duty with the Lord Mayor both in London and abroad. This service with the Reserves dates from the old concept of Citizen Soldiers, the 'trained bands' of the Tudors. To demonstrate this continuing obligation to defend the City and the Country, most Livery Companies 'adopt' a naval ship, a regiment or squadron. The Stationers, for example, 'adopted' the Corps of Royal Marines. To them has been granted the Freedom of the City. They have the right to march through the streets with 'bayonets fixed, drums beating and Colours flying'. They are also affiliated to St Lawrence Jewry, thereby confirming the Church's belief that 'it is lawful for Christian men, at the commandment of the Magistrate, to wear weapons, and serve in the wars'. The Livery honours the profession of arms, in the defence of the realm.

The Idea of The Livery

The practice of religion

Although individuals may not be 'religious', the Livery is most apparently so when all companies attend an annual service at St Paul's Cathedral on the Friday before Holy week. The Cathedral is then packed. All the pomp and ceremony of processions and music proclaim the importance of the occasion. Less in number, but similar in intent, is the attendance at St Lawrence Jewry on Michaelmas Day of all Masters, as representatives of their companies seeking divine guidance before they process across Guildhall Yard to Common Hall for the election of the Lord Mayor. Companies appoint Chaplains who have no difficulty in identifying with their spirit. Services are arranged, usually in connection with the election or installation of a new Master.

That, in turn, is often dated by the Saints Day kept by the neighbourhood church in whose honour the Livery is dedicated. The City motto is said by the Lord Mayor as a prayer at the beginning of each meeting of Common Council, and often by the Master of the Company at Court meetings. Grace is said before meat and sung afterwards. The City flag wears the Cross, with St Paul's Sword of the Spirit in one quarter. The totality of life is expressed in its all-embracing motto: *Domine Dirige Nos*. No Liveryman is unaware that the worship of Almighty God is a deeply engrained part of the life of his Company, and that the pursuit of excellence in the service of the community is of the essence of the idea of the Livery.

Historically, the medieval Livery Companies, whose ethos has been analysed, derive from the Anglo-Saxon fraternities which existed for mutual assistance and religious observance, as well as for guarding the standards and conditions of their trade. Their incorporation by Royal Prerogative in a Charter was a much coveted status for such a body enjoyed perpetual succession. It could own property immune from the hazards and penalties of life and death which could befall its individual members. This has led to the accumulation of the wealth which has enabled the Companies to play their unique role in our contemporary society. The term Livery is a relic of feudalism when barons, prelates and monastic houses granted clothing and an allowance of food and wine to their dependents. The style of clothing was influenced by the monastic orders and has evolved into the gown and hood. Early in their history, the Companies individually adopted distinctive colours of Livery.

The Idea of The Livery

The Association of Livery Masters 1985
Mansion House 16 June 1988
Annual Ladies Luncheon

    GRACE

    No man can serve two masters, so says the Good Book
    But when Masters are two for a penny, Lord, do have a look
    For you'll see them underfed, though not famished
    Untoasted nowadays and called 'Past'
    But asking your blessing
    Each other addressing
    As 'Incomparables' of the '85 class.

Livery Masters 1984–5 Associations
22 October 1992 Bakers' Hall
Combined Ladies Guest Night

    GRACE

    We're Masters past
    Never known to fast
    Always grateful for what is good
    Like friends of old and well-served food
    But when, dear Lord, it's specially bles't
    The wine turns vintage — we like that best.

                                                             Amen

Livery Companies
in order of precedence

Precedence determined by the Court of Aldermen in 1516

1 Mercers
2 Grocers
3 Drapers
4 Fishmongers
5 Goldsmiths
6 Skinners
7 Merchant Taylors
8 Haberdashers
9 Salters
10 Ironmongers
11 Vintners
12 Clothworkers
13 Dyers
14 Brewers
15 Leathersellers
16 Pewterers
17 Barbers
18 Cutlers
19 Bakers
20 Waxchandlers
21 Tallowchandlers
22 Armourers & Brasiers
23 Girdlers
24 Butchers
25 Saddlers
26 Carpenters
27 Cordwainers
28 Painter Stainers
29 Curriers
30 Masons
31 Plumbers
32 Innholders
33 Founders
34 Poulters
35 Cooks
36 Coopers
37 Tylers & Bricklayers
38 Bowyers
39 Fletchers
40 Blacksmiths
41 Joiners
42 Weavers
43 Woolmen
44 Scriveners
45 Fruiterers
46 Plaisterers
47 Stationers
48 Broderers
49 Upholders
50 Musicians
51 Turners
52 Basketmakers
53 Glaziers
54 Horners
55 Farriers
56 Paviors
57 Loriners
58 Apothecaries
59 Shipwrights
60 Spectaclemakers
61 Clockmakers
62 Glovers

Livery Companies in order of precedence

63 Feltmakers
64 Framework Knitters
65 Needlemakers
66 Gardeners
67 Tinplate Workers
68 Wheelwrights
69 Distillers
70 Pattenmakers
71 Glass Sellers
72 Coachmakers & Coach Harness Makers
73 Gunmakers
74 Gold & Silver Wyre Drawers
75 Makers of Playing Cards
76 Fanmakers
77 Carmen
78 Master Mariners
79 Solicitors
80 Farmers
81 Air Pilots & Air Navigators
82 Tobacco Pipe Makers & Tobacco Blenders
83 Furniture Makers
84 Scientific Instrument Makers
85 Chartered Surveyors
86 Chartered Accountants Technologists
87 Chartered Secretaries and Administrators
88 Builders Merchants
89 Launderers
90 Marketors
91 Actuaries
92 Insurers
93 Arbitrators
94 Engineers
95 Fuellers
96 Lightmongers
97 Environmental Cleaners
98 Chartered Architects
99 Constructors
100 Information Technologists

The Shrievalty

Only one who has served the office of Sheriff can become Lord Mayor: so states an Ordinance of 1385. The Shrievalty is thus pivotal to the structure of the City's corporate life. It is the proving ground for promotion to the Mayoralty on the one hand and, on the other, it is the evidence of the historic independence of the Livery in Common Hall to elect its Officials. The office predates the Mayoralty. William the Norman, William I, addressed the Charter of 1067 to Geoffrey de Mandeville, the first Sheriff after the Conquest, while Geoffrey was still in his previous office of Portreeve. This historic document, the original of which is a treasured possession of the Corporation, confirmed to the citizens of London their pre-Conquest rights, including that of having a civic head: a Portreeve. (That title was incorporated in the larger Shire-reeve, eventually becoming Sheriff.) Sheriffs are, therefore, in origin Royal Officials: the Queen's Sheriffs appointed, in those days, to collect the Royal revenues. In the rest of the country, they are still appointed — 'pricked' — by the Monarch. In the City, they are elected by the Livery: two each year, one of whom, by convention, is already an Alderman. Later, the elections are approved by the Monarch. This ancient practice was confirmed by Act of Parliament in 1725. The Monarch long accepted and recognised that the Livery consisted of responsible citizens who could be trusted to elect fit and proper persons to collect even the Royal revenues and to dispense justice. The Sheriffs now have no executive power, but are visible holders of an office that has evolved from the days of the Conquest. They are witness to that unique City feature — the electoral power of the Livery. Their election takes place in Common Hall on Mid-Summer Day. They assume office on the vigil of Michaelmas Day (28 September) to be in position at the election on that day of the Lord Mayor. They have the invaluable experience of being 'trained' during the next six weeks by the reigning Lord Mayor.

Some holders of the office think the Shrievalty 'honour and enough'. They have no wish, for one reason or another, to go on to the Mayoralty, so do not aspire to be an Alderman. Such Sheriffs are

The Shrievalty

usually referred to as Lay, as distinct from Aldermanic. Aldermen serving the office are therefore on the ladder of possible selection for the Mayoralty. Before the War, Sheriffs were rewarded with a knighthood, but not now. They gain the honour of doing the job for its own sake — and the expense of it! One of the expenses is a share in the cost of the Lord Mayor's Banquet: the Lord Mayor pays half, the other half is borne equally by each Sheriff. Expenses are considerable and only partly funded by City's cash. Nobody would voluntarily undertake the year unless he was personally willing to put his hand deep into his own pocket.

The other expense is time. Time keeps the Sheriffs on duty, more or less continuously as they attend on the Lord Mayor for all his official functions. They are seen dressed in knee breeches and buckled shoes, frock coat with lace jabots and cuffs, surmounted by a chain and badge containing their coat of arms and other related insignia. The badge is usually a magnificent example of the jeweller's craft, and is the gift of each Sheriff's friends from within the Livery and the Ward. A Sheriff so attired will spend his every other day at the Old Bailey. There, trailing some of his judicial past, he opens the Court on behalf of the Lord Mayor and is present throughout the session. While there, he also entertains the Judges to lunch and gives a few chosen friends the immense pleasure of joining them. No guest ever forgets sitting at lunch with the scarlet or black robed and legally wigged Judges, enjoying their table talk. In the evening, both Sheriffs, often with their ladies, accompany the Lord Mayor on his dining duties. Frequently, they return to their suite of rooms at the Old Bailey for the night, being driven in their official limousines. One or other, or both, will be with the Lord Mayor when he makes goodwill visits in this country and abroad; particularly so, when, at the request of the Foreign Office, and acting as an Ambassador Extraordinary, he makes a prolonged visit to a distant country during the summer months. Sheriffs form an essential part of the colourful party which catches the eye in foreign parts and drums up business for the City and prestige for the country generally.

It is, of course, desirable that a close relationship should exist between the Lord Mayor and the two Sheriffs. His fellow Alderman, the Aldermanic Sheriff, will be well known to him. The Lay Sheriff, who may be any Freeman of the City, is often a personal friend of the Lord Mayor. The Lord Mayor can nominate any such friends provided their names are announced in the Court of Aldermen between 14 March

The Shrievalty

and 14 May for selection by the Livery on Mid-Summer Day. After the Shrieval year, the testing year for the Alderman, it has been customary for Aldermen who have 'passed the chair' to let the Aldermanic Sheriff know whether or not they think that he has got what it takes to make a successful Lord Mayor. If they indicate privately to him that they will not vote for him, he will, of course, be disappointed; but he will be saved the future embarrassment of public rejection. In this very urbane way, the City enables the Alderman to drop out quietly in the course of the following year. It is always hoped that there will be three or four Aldermen who have served the office of Sheriff so that more than one will be available for the Mayoralty. Accidents do happen. If the reserve numbers are short, two Aldermen will be asked to serve in the same year and there will be no Lay Sheriff.

A Liveryman of the Shipwrights' Company, John Hart, became Lay Sheriff to his lifelong friend Sir Peter Gadsden, as Lord Mayor. John Hart was a Scottish Rugger International. With his wife, Anne, he served a memorable year as Sheriff. In the Company, we gave a lunch for him.

GRACE

We have chosen a Shipwright for Sheriff
He is one of our own kith and kin
So we ask thee, dear Lord, to bless him
With your Grace as our meal we begin

Amen

GRACE: AT LUNCH AFTER THE YEAR'S SHRIEVALTY

As we celebrate a Shrievalty
Of undetected crime
And assemble here in fealty
For the last of John Hart's wine
We ask a special blessing, Lord, on what the menu says
  we've got
While praying that the Mayoralty may be this
  Shipwright's lot.

Amen

Addendum
For John Hart, the office was 'honour and enough'. He was a loss to the Mayoralty.

Graces on Some Livery Company Occasions

There follow some chapters on the history of various Companies to which I have been Chaplain; sometimes for a Master's year, on his personal invitation; at others, as permanent Company Chaplain. Graces, therefore, tend to be few or many.

THE WORSHIPFUL COMPANY OF GROCERS
Charter 1428
Order of precedence: second to the Mercers

The Company emerged from the Guild of Pepperers in 1376. The name probably is derived from the medieval word meaning one who buys and sells by the gross: a wholesale merchant. The original business of the Company was in the control of the spice trade of London. This it did until superseded by the Customs and Excise after the Great Fire.

Halls have stood on the site in Princes Street since 1427. The fifth survived the War but was destroyed by fire in 1965, rebuilt and opened in 1970. The walls are lined with crimson silk and are complemented in colour by the three Venetian chandeliers. The Hall is dominated by the Oscar Nemon bust of the Queen Mother; while the great feature of the Library, with further cases elsewhere, is the Walter Hale Glass Collection. There are many other notable gifts that enhance this very sumptuous Hall.

Livery Dinner: Grocers' Hall, 1974
Master: Robin MacKenzie

> GRACE
> It's not slugs and snails
> And puppy dog's tails
> But cloves and spice
> And all things nice
> That old Grocers were made of.
> Today, too, bless them, Lord
> And all that we are about to partake of . . . .
>
> Amen

Graces on Some Grocers' Company Occasions

Livery Dinner, 14 January 1980
Master: The Hon. Sir Clive Bossom Bt

> GRACE
>
> It's a blessing we ask as we sit down to dine
> On most promising victuals and good vintage wine
> So we stand now as Grocers accustomed to pray
> And ask you to hear, Lord, the things that we say
> For we know that our peppers and spice will be bettered by Grace
> And have no envy of Mercers for their pride of place
> Just for now: for it's we who the Lord Mayor of London this day
> Have the honour of hosting in Bossom's masterly way.

Private dinner given by the Master
2 July 1986, his 10th wedding anniversary
Master: Alexander Sparkes

> GRACE
>
> None of us would be here, Lord, unless you'd contrived
> Ten years ago for Alexander to take Serena as bride
> They've been fruitful and multiplied in Emma and Hugo
> And he's now Master of Grocers as well you do know
> So please bless them both
> Re-affirming their troth
> And us too, dear Lord, as we sit down to dine
> Rejoicing with them in this anniversary wine.
>
> Amen

I had married Alexander to Serena Fairfax and baptised both of their children. During his year as Master, I attended various functions. At the end of it, he brought his Company to St Lawrence Jewry for a service of Thanksgiving before the Election Feast.

THE WORSHIPFUL COMPANY OF MERCHANT TAYLORS
Charter 1327
Order of precedence: 6/7

One of the Great Twelve Companies, seniority at sixth being shared in alternate years with the Skinners by the judgement of Mayor Billesden in 1484. 'To be at sixes and sevens' is the current expression derived

Graces on Some Merchant Taylors' Company Occasions

from this incident in City life, both Companies having originally received their Charter on the same day. In 1516, the Court of Aldermen determined the Order of precedence which now applies.

The Hall: 30 Threadneedle Street
Destroyed during World War 2, it was rebuilt by Sir Albert Richardson. Prior to that, it had been the only pre-Fire Livery Hall and had traces of its medieval origin. The Parlour has been rebuilt as a replica of the 17th century original.

There is a two manual organ in the Hall. It is thought that the National Anthem was first sung here and conducted by its author, John Bull.

1980
In the year that Sir Charles Alexander Bt was Master, I acted as his Chaplain, preaching at his Installation Service and on the occasion of the annual Wylford service at St Helen's Bishopsgate. His father was Lord Mayor in 1944–5 and his mother was the daughter of Sir Charles Collett, Lord Mayor 1933–4. He was the nephew of Sir Kingsley Collett, my Churchwarden. I was caught up in their joint family affairs from early days in the City and greatly enjoyed the special relationship of Chaplain.

The Annual Reconciliation Dinner
Merchant Taylors' Hall
Date: 29 June 1982

> GRACE
> Though we set our lives at six and seven
> Mayor Billesden defined a way to heaven
> Ordaining as a means to keep us sweet
> A blessing we should ask on what we eat
> May that friendship now be fostered in the Loving Cup of Wine
> As together at this table we and Skinners sit to dine.
> Amen

Graces on Some Haberdashers' Company Occasions

THE WORSHIPFUL COMPANY OF HABERDASHERS
Charter 1448
Order of precedence: 8th among the Great Twelve

Hall: Staining Lane, EC2

The present Hall, built to the design of Major W Ash in 1954–6, stands on the site of previous halls that date from the 15th century. All have been destroyed by fire.

It is generally accepted that the name comes from the early English hapertas which was the personal garment of coarse woollen cloth worn under armour. Haberdashery came to include most items of personal wear. The Company controlled that trade until the 17th century.

The present activity of the Company is an excellent example of the exercise of Livery benevolence. It educates over 5,000 children in the eight schools of its various foundations in London (Haberdashers' Aske's at Elstree with 1350 pupils is the largest), Monmouth, Newport (Shropshire) and Bunbury (Cheshire). It maintains 42 almshouses and is the trustee of over 100 other charities.

With its commitment to the academic life, the Company likes its traditional Grace to be said in Latin:

GRACE

> Benedic, Domine, quaesumus Ecclesiae sanctae tuae,
> Reginae nostrae augustissimae, necnon et societati
> reverendae Haberdasherorum; et concede ut, salubriter
> his tuis donis enutriti, tibi debitum obsequium
> praestare valeamus; per Jesum Christum Dominum
> nostrum.
>
> Amen

When challenged by a Liveryman on one occasion for offering Grace in a language which they did not understand, I told the story of being similarly taxed by the Commander in a naval mess when, as a young Chaplain, I had said Benedictus Benedicat. A Roman Catholic Admiral, Admiral A. C. C. Miers VC, who was a guest, came to my aid: 'My dear Commander, that Grace wasn't given to you, but to Someone who perfectly well understands that language'. The more normal version, which I frequently adapt to other Companies, is:

> Preserve, O Lord, the Church, the Queen and the
> Worshipful Company of Haberdashers, and bless these
> gifts to our use and ourselves to thy service.
>
> Amen

Graces on Some Girdlers' Company Occasions

I was made Free of the City and a Liveryman also of the Company on 24 July 1970. My parchment scroll is romantically signed by Richard Whittington, at that time Chamberlain of the City. I am proud that it is my mother Company. A Loving Cup, a silver gilt goblet, designed by Gerald Benny, was presented to me on my retirement. Constantly in use, it is pledged to the many friendships I made in a Company which was virtually my parish.

THE WORSHIPFUL COMPANY OF GIRDLERS
Charter 1449
Order of precedence: 23

Hall: Basinghall Street, EC2
Built substantially on the original site devised to the Company in 1431, the Hall stands in its own prize-winning City garden. The previous Hall was destroyed during the War. Its present replacement was built in 1961 to the plan of the late Ted Fleming, Liveryman, and to the design of Cedric Ripley. It was decorated by Malcolm Sherrard, Liveryman, who was one of the top post-war designers, skilled in the use of the best fabrics, such as he used in the Hall. It is ideally functional, with all the charm and domestic atmosphere of a lived-in country house.

Central to the scheme of decoration, and occupying one wall of the Livery Hall, is the Lahore carpet. Commissioned and presented to the Company in 1634 by Robert Bell, it has been mercifully saved from the destruction of the previous Halls.

The Company have the honour to present the Girdle, or Sword Belt, for the Sword of State at each Sovereign's coronation. This is in recognition of the original craft of making the girdles, particularly their metal work, which were worn outside a tunic or gown. From such girdles were suspended the purse, wallet or side arms. The craft has long since fallen into abeyance, but its Liverymen come from families with historic connections to the craft and with the City. In 1216, Benet Le Seinturer (Girdler) was made Sheriff of London (The Shrievalty *q.v.*).

The Arms embody three girdle-irons and the crest is a figure of St Lawrence. The instrument of their trade is a punning allusion to their patron saint and the gridiron on which he was slowly roasted. During the Diocletian persecutions, when the Roman authorities asked Lawrence, the treasurer of the church in Rome, to hand over the church's treasures (of plate and silver) he paraded the lepers, the halt

Graces on Some Girdlers' Company Occasions

and the blind saying that they were the treasures of the Church. For this 'levity', he was martyred. The medieval hagiographers gave him the last triumphant word: 'You can turn me over, I'm done on that side'. Fittingly, the gridiron is incorporated in the weather vane of St Lawrence Jewry, the Company's church.

Benevolence is expressed through the two Company Almshouses and particularly in the three scholarships worth £10,000 each, granted annually to New Zealand scholars at Cambridge. Since 1954, there has grown up, through St Lawrence Jewry, a special relationship which is observed on Waitangi Day. There is a church service, followed by a tea party at the hall and a dinner in the evening given by the New Zealand Society usually in the River Room at the Savoy and attended by the Master and Wardens.

This relationship was brought about by the Vicar, the Revd. W P Besley, 1920–35. He spent a sabbatical in New Zealand and was cured of TB. In gratitude, he made an upper room in the church (now the drawing room of the Vicarage) into a club room for nurses from New Zealand. The special relationship was further cemented by Bill Jordan, a City policeman and member of St Lawrence Jewry, who emigrated in the '30s to New Zealand: he was active there as a Trade Unionist and returned as a member of Churchill's wartime Commonwealth Cabinet. He was made a Liveryman of the Company.

The cellars contain the wines in which the Company have become connoisseurs through the skill and interest in their selection. Colonel Lionel Dennis, chairman for the past 25 years of the wine committee, always provides a written description of the wines chosen for Court and Livery dinners. A typical description of the wines chosen for the Court Ladies Luncheon, 10 December 1987, follows.

Gewurztraminer 1976
The Gewurztraminer together with the Riesling are the two finest wines coming from Alsace, the most northerly table wine growing region of France, and the wines from this district are all marketed by the name of the grape variety.

This particular grape, the Gewurztraminer, is without doubt the most individual tasting white wine produced in the whole of France. In good years, of which 1976 is one, it produces a delicious fruity wine, full of flavour and with a touch of violets on the nose. It is so distinctive in taste that you either adore it, like John Rutherford, or you prefer the drier and more elegant whites, as does Lord Brentford. However, on a

Graces on Some Girdlers' Company Occasions

cold December day, it will certainly be much in favour with the ladies and certain members of the Court.

Chapelle Chambertin 1982
Chapelle is one of the more delicate wines of this northerly commune of the Cote du Nuits. Generally, the wines of Gevrey are full bodied and robust, assertive and strictly masculine. While those from Chapelle share these qualities, they have a lightness, a fruitiness sometimes, and a certain finesse which tends to set them apart.

The red burgundies in the 1982 vintage were wines of above average quality which are maturing fairly quickly, and this is the first time the Court has had of sampling this particular year and coming from one of the greatest domaines and growers, Clair Dau.

Rieussec 1976
A Bordeaux white wine from the commune of Fargues in the district of Sauternes. Full bodied, but less subtle, it is contiguous with Chateau D'Yquem and is officially classed as a First Growth of Sauternes in the 1855 classification.

The 1976 vintage in Sauternes was an extremely fine one and should now be showing well — rich on the palate, but will continue to improve.

Fonseca 1970
One of the great Port Houses which has consistently in the declared port vintages of this century produced classic full-bodied rich wines with the ability to improve with age. As the 1966 and 1963 are now becoming scarce, the Company is now beginning to drink the 1970 vintage. The year is an excellent one for vintage port, the wines being extremely full-bodied and rich.

>GRACE
>
>The Company motto is: 'Give thanks to God'
>It is incorporated in the invariable Grace:
>
>'For these and all his mercies, give thanks to God'.
>
>   Amen

Graces on Some Fletchers' Company Occasions

THE WORSHIPFUL COMPANY OF FLETCHERS
Order of precedence: 39

Their Hall is 3 Cloth Street, EC1. It is shared with the Worshipful Company of Farmers and was opened on Tuesday 9 June 1987 by Her Royal Highness, The Princess Royal.

Fletchers is one of the few newly built Halls. Since the War, some have been rebuilt on old sites: others have been incorporated in large office blocks; others in buildings adapted to this new use and shared with other companies. This Hall, designed by Michael Twigg Brown and Partners, has been purpose built for the two companies: one ancient, the other modern. Most companies want a home of their own: sharing one is perhaps the best compromise, as the Farmers and Fletchers have done.

Luncheon following the official opening, 9 June 1987
Master: A N Taylor

GRACE

Dear Lord
When Farmers and Fletchers fraternise
To build a Hall of this elegant size
And a Princess sheds such a royal ray
Over the opening proceedings of this special day
We pray thy Grace on our food and our wine
And a blessing each time that we sit down to dine.

Amen

The Ladies Banquet
Master: Maurice Hart, Esq.
3 February 1993

GRACE

Its a Fletchers request, Lord, that we pray Thee
For we have as special guests, the Lord Mayor and his Lady
All other wives and sweethearts are delighted that she
Defeated young Jehu and retains her beauty
So with our thanks for all mercies as we sit down to dine
We ask a Blessing on our ladies, our food and our wine.

Amen

Graces on Some Fletchers' Company Occasions

Note
On the eve of the Lord Mayor's Show, the Lady Mayoress was knocked down by a motorbike messenger and badly injured.

The Farmers' and Fletchers' Hall, 30 April 1992
Installation Dinner
Master: Maurice Hart

> GRACE
>
> What a pleasure it is when we Fletchers dine
> In the new Master's name which sounds like a sign
> Of all friendship and love
> That comes from above
> A special blessing please, Lord, on his food and his wine.
>
> Amen

Ladies Banquet, Wednesday 3 February 1988: the first in the Hall
Guest of Honour: The Lord Mayor,
  the Rt Hon Sir Greville Spratt GBE
Master: A N Taylor

> GRACE
>
> Fletchers and Toxophilites we made a martial band
> With bowmen who once fought in defence of this our land
> And we've always helped boy Cupid with what he flights for darts
> For he has brought us here tonight with our wives and sweetest hearts
> To sit down with the Lord Mayor
> And say a special prayer
> For a prandial Grace on us, on each and all
> That we'll enjoy our goodies in this new and splendid Hall.
>
> Amen

There followed a round of applause! Gareth Daniel, in replying for the guests, a professional at this task, said that of the many such dinners he had attended, he had never before heard a Grace receive a standing

Graces on Some Fletchers' Company Occasions

ovation! A little later in the course of the dinner, Vera Brown, wife of a past Master, delighted me with her personal response:

> 'Dear Basil, your talent for speaking in verse
> I wish I could copy — but quite the reverse.
> When Livery dinners are set on the table
> And wine flows abundantly, I am not able
> To bring wit to bear on the subject of rhyme
> So my salutations come later in time
> I think you do splendidly, naught could be clearer
> God bless and inspire you. Yours faithfully Vera.'

Later, she presented herself at my chair while the coffee was being served. That is a time when the Ladies and Gentlemen can move about in what is referred to as a cold weather routine. I relished kissing her on both cheeks. The whole evening was a great ego trip — further enhanced when the Master, Tony Taylor, made me feel very much part of his and the Fletcher family. He told the assembled company that I had sent his father on his journey Home: had married him and christened his two children. I am always sorry for parsons who think that their job is sitting on committees, shuffling synod papers and politicising Inner Cities. Nothing, to my mind, compares with the privilege of sharing with other humans the great and sacred mysteries of their lives.

I am mindful of the year that I served as Chaplain to Vera's husband, Joseph Brown, as Master.

Date: 24 April 1986
Installation dinner: Innholders' Hall

GRACE

> The Master looks splendid in his chain and gown
> So he should for he's our own Joseph Brown
> In him the Fletchers have done themselves proud
> For he speaks well — and is equally loud.
> In making requests
> For his Livery and guests
> That when they happily sit down to dine
> They'll enjoy both their food and this good vintage wine
> Dear Lord we thank you.
>
> Amen

Graces on Some Fletchers' Company Occasions

Stationers' Hall
Ladies Banquet
13 February 1987, Eve of St Valentine

> GRACE
>
> 'Wives and sweethearts' was the toast at sea, we always drank with zest
> 'May they never meet' Navalwise we added as our usual jest
> But on Valentine's Eve they are all welcome here in the romance of Stationers' Hall
> And on this excellent food and the choicest of wine
> A blessing is asked 'ere we sit down to dine.
> We know that the Fletchers would all have it so
> Specially for the Browns: the lovely Vera and Joe.

Fletchers sometimes used Stationers' Hall for their Ladies Banquet before they achieved their own Hall. The naval touch coloured the Grace somewhat as the Stationers had adopted, as their Services' commitment, the Corps of Royal Marines. For Livery dinners, they usually went to the Innholders, and always enjoyed moving around other halls according to the size of their guest requirement.

Joseph Brown was a very eloquent and ready speaker. He had been Deputy Chairman of the GLC before joining Common Council where he became Chief Commoner. He was also Lay Sheriff in 1977. In that capacity, and as Master, he added distinction to the office by a sure use of the English language.

In a previous year, I had been Chaplain to the Master, Charles Coward. I was also Chaplain to his son, Clive, for the year 1988–9. Fletchers are one of the Companies where the Chaplain is not the Company's chaplain but the Master's appointment, and so for the year only. It is a good variant as many Masters have brothers or other relatives who are parsons. Some have a special relationship with their local Vicar and wish to have him associated with them in their year of office. I have enjoyed that role on a number of occasions. I prefer, though, to be the Company chaplain and, over the years, to build up a pastoral relationship with its Liverymen. Clerks know that I like to be seated next to Liverymen, not guests; and preferably below the salt, so that I get to know as many as possible individually. Especially was this so when I was a Guild vicar in the City: having a church, but no

Graces on Some Fletchers' Company Occasions

parishioners and no Sunday worship. Among other things, that made it possible to stay for the weekend with Liverymen friends and preach for their vicar. Establishing good relations between the village and the City was of value too, especially when the City was to rob the vicar of a marriage that often, for a number of reasons, was better held in London.

Ladies Banquet, 6 February 1980
Guest of Honour: The Rt Hon The Lord Mayor,
  Sir Peter Gadsden GBE
Ironmongers' Hall
Master: Charles Coward

> GRACE
>
> With his arrows of desire
> In his chariot of fire
> Blake prayed for England
> And here, O Lord, those arrow makers
> Welcome all to be partakers
> Of the pleasures of this green and pleasant land
> Dependent now, as always, on the blessings of Your
>   hand.
>
> Amen

This sentiment had a 16th century precursor:
> And thus I pray God that al Fletchers getting their lyvynge truly and al archers vsynge shootynge honestly, and al manner of men that favour artillery, may lyve continuallye in healthe and meriness, obeying theyr prince as they shulde and loving God as they ought, to whom for al things be al honour and glorye for ever.
>
> Amen
>
> (From the *Toxophilus* of Roger Ascham 1545)

At his Installation on Tuesday 12 April 1986, Clive Coward, son of Charles, made his masterly speech wholly in doggerel — it duly provided the postscript to this rather egotistical reflection on some Fletcher occasion . . . .

> 'Arrangements beforehand were made by the Clerk
> Whose legendary efficiency was up to the mark
> He crossed all his 't's' and his 'i's' all had dots on
> And we opened with Grace by the Rev. Basil Watson.'

Graces on Some Fletchers' Company Occasions

Court dinner on 21 July 1988
Master: Clive Coward

> GRACE
>
> Fletchers have a poet as Master
> Whose verse keeps them pealing with laughter
> But, dear Lord, what one hears
> Are the contrasting fears
> Lest the Grace makes this meal a disaster.
>
>   Amen

Golden Wedding Anniversary
Charles and Cathy Coward
Lunch given at the Farmers' & Fletchers' Hall, 9 July 1985

> GRACE
>
> Today, Lord, we gather with special intent
> To help two good friends gratefully observe their life's journey's event
> They've been cheered by their Clive over most of its miles
> With Frances, JJ, Tamsin and Giles
> But our Charles could not have achieved it, not even he
> Without the enduring love of his devoted Cathy.
>
>   Amen

Farmers' and Fletchers' Hall, 24 April 1990
Livery Dinner
Master: John Redgrave

> GRACE
>
> Before Fletchers take wine
> They ask a blessing divine
> On all they're about to enjoy
> Their youngest Freeman too
> Of whom they've made much ado
> Now raises his voice
> To be heard to rejoice
> And pledge to be loyal and true.

This personal reference followed a meeting of the Court at which Fletchers honoured me with their Freedom. It was a signal honour as

Graces on Some Fletchers' Company Occasions

I was not the Company Chaplain but had been Chaplain to a number of Masters over the years.

Farmers' and Fletchers' Hall, 23 January 1991
A joint dinner of Fletchers and Bowyers

> GRACE
>
> Every arrow needs its bow
> Pictures of Cupid show that's so
> Surely then tonight there's approval divine
> As again Bowyers with Fletchers sit down to dine
> May such shining virtue, O Lord
> Be richly blessed at this unity Board.

Fletchers and Bowyers had sadly fallen out some 500 years ago. This dinner marked a stage in the thawing-out process of those strained relations.

Farmers' and Fletchers' Hall, 6 February 1991
Ladies Banquet
Master: John Redgrave

> GRACE
>
> What pleasure it is, Lord, when we Fletchers dine
> As we're superbly looked after with good food and fine wine
> On that our reputation for hospitality rests
> Dispensed in our Hall to our well-chosen guests
> In Lent moreover from such delights it would be hard to abstain
> A special blessing then please on those who'll be under considerable strain.
>
>   Amen

Farmers' and Fletchers' Hall, 14 March 1991
Court Dinner:
Guest of Honour: The Rt Hon The Lord Mayor,
   Sir Alexander Graham

> GRACE
>
> Their loss is our gain and delight
> As we've got the Lord Mayor for tonight

Graces on Some Loriners' Company Occasions

He's had to forego the Gulf and our boys
But now comes to Fletchers for our culinary joys
Lord kindly bless chef's haggis-free dishes
May the evening fulfil our good Master's wishes.

Amen

The Lord Mayor, Sir Alexander Graham, a Scot, and by this time halfway through his Mayoralty, had been over-indulged with a surfeit of haggis. He had been unable to visit the troops in the Gulf as D-Day there was imminent.

THE WORSHIPFUL COMPANY OF LORINERS
Charters: First Charter 1261
Charter of Incorporation 1712
Order of precedence: 57

A Loriner is a craftsman almost unknown today except to the initiated. He was a bridle-maker, Lorimer in the Norman French, in turn deriving from the Latin Lorum meaning 'a bridle'. By the 17th century, Loriner was the accepted use.

In essence, the first man who learned how essential the bridle is to the control and comfort of his horse was such a craftsman. The modern technician is only excelled by the owner of the hands and fingers which hold the reins. The various types of bridles and bits are often classified according to a Past Master, James W White:

1 Snaffles   4 The Gags
2 Pelhams   5 The Bitless Group
3 Curbs

Livery Dinner: 29 January 1980
Vintners' Hall
Master: Keith Vartan

GRACE

Preserve, O Lord, the Church, the Queen and all her subjects
Spur us in her service
Bridle our tongues from evil by the good fellowship of the evening

Graces on Some Loriners' Company Occasions

That, with Thanksgiving, we may enjoy
The Bits and Pieces of Thy creation of which
We are about to partake.

Amen

Livery Lunch: December 1979
Barber Surgeons' Hall
Master: John Hovey

Lunch followed the Court Meeting at which HRH The Princess Anne — the Princess Royal — was clothed in the Livery. When introduced to her before lunch, I expressed the hope that she would not mind a passing reference in the Grace. 'As long as it doesn't spoil the food', she said with a permissive chuckle.

GRACE

We're asking a blessing, O Lord, on a menu
That's in tasty accord with this modern venue
And also we pray
In a Loriner's way
That our bits and bridles and spurs
May be usefully hers
Whom we've clothed in our Livery today.

Amen

Livery Dinner: Installation 1986
Vintners' Hall
Master: R J Bowman

GRACE

It's Loriners, O Lord, who at Vintners
Eat the first of their new Master's dinners
He's now asked for Grace as we sit down to dine
And further requests
For his Livery and guests
Enjoyment, not least of his wine.

Amen

Graces on Some Shipwrights' Company Occasions

THE WORSHIPFUL COMPANY OF SHIPWRIGHTS
Order of precedence: 59

The craft of the Shipwright has played such an unique part in national life, both in peace and in war, that it is natural that the Royal Family should be closely associated with the Company. H M The Queen is Patron. The Duke of Edinburgh is Permanent Master and the Prince of Wales is a Liveryman and Member of the Court of Assistants. Queen Elizabeth, The Queen Mother, is an honorary Freeman. In welcoming Prince Charles to the Court, the Duke had playfully discoursed on the nature of nepotism! Whereupon, in reply to the Toast, the Prince of Wales addressed him as Permanent Father. The continuing banter on both occasions was revealing and endearing. The Company rejoices in this royal and privileged association.

It is natural, too, that is should be one of the larger Liveries. There is a permitted membership of 500. Until comparatively recently, a third were builders, a third owners and a third seafarers. Those proportions are changing dramatically with the demise of so much of the industry and of shipping generally. More than half are in the Maritime services with the emphasis being on the active and retired list of the Royal Navy.

It was a great joy then to me to be invited to be Chaplain in 1974 by the late Sir Leslie Bowes (past Chairman of the Royal Mail Line) on the recommendation of Sir Charles Trinder, past Lord Mayor. My 26 years in the Royal Navy meant that I joined with a good deal of flying speed in knowing members. I have been able to build on and extend many friendships — Admiral Sir Morgan Morgan-Giles, Prime Warden 1987–8, was my Captain in HMS Vernon some 30 years ago and, during that time, I have been involved with his family on all pastoral occasions and have recently shared many thoughts with him on the nature and function of the Livery. Morgan M Giles had been Captain of HMS Belfast in the Far East on her last commission. He was then instrumental in having her preserved and brought up river to the pool of London to be a maritime museum. I have committed the ashes of many Liverymen 'to the deep' from her quarter-deck. He invited me to be her Chaplain. David Pelly and Sir Charles Alexander, Shipwrights, gave much time to fostering a Sea Cadet unit on board.

The Company was established as a London brotherhood as far back as 1260, working in yards just east of London Bridge. They formed themselves into a fraternity in honour of St Simon and St Jude in 1456.

The Painted Hall, Greenwich: Trafalgar Night Dinner. Officers are seated for Grace at the request of the BBC who were broadcasting the proceedings.

Graces on Some Shipwrights' Company Occasions

They only applied to the Court of Aldermen for an authorised Livery in 1782 having strangely lost their Charter after winning a bitter legal battle with a rival shipping company. Meanwhile, the yards were moved to Ratcliffe and Wapping, then the centre of the craft. The Company is now housed in Ironmongers' Hall at the South West corner of Barbican. Substantial though this Hall is, built in the Tudor style in 1925, it is not large enough to take all the Company — maximum seating is 170. An Annual Banquet when the Livery invite guests is usually held in Plaisterers' Hall on the opposite side of London Wall. Glaziers and other halls are used. Ladies come to the Civic Banquet traditionally held at Mansion House and to the Court lunch at Trinity House. The Installation dinner is held every second year at Greenwich in the Painted Hall. It must be one of the most magnificent and sought after Banqueting scenes in London. Shipwrights are one of the few Companies honoured to exercise hospitality in it. Going back for such occasions always fills me with the sweet smelling savour of what I regard as 'success'! Early in my naval career, I was appointed Chaplain to the College, then an academy for sub lieutenants and a staff and war college for more senior ranks. I was then one of two Chaplains in the Branch with an honours degree in history, entitled therefore to be borne on the College books as a tutor, though not as Chaplain. Chaplains could only be borne in ships and establishments of 600 souls. Admiral Sir Julian Oswald, GCB now First Sea Lord, obviously benefitted by being one of my tutor set though, sadly, I lost him to Rome in the course of his later career. It is typical of him that he wrote to tell me so at the time, and has now kindly contributed a most gracious foreword. The likes of the late Admiral Sir David Hallifax and Admiral Sir Sandy Woodward recently Commander in Chief, Naval Home Command and of Falklands fame, had to listen to me spinning many a yarn from the great pulpit in the College Chapel!

It was my privilege in 1952 to be entrusted with the restoration of the Chapel after its War damage and to re-arrange it for Prayer Book worship. It was a three year task which brought me in touch with distinguished artists and craftsmen as well as David Eccles, then Minister of Works, who greatly encouraged me, promising the necessary funds. (Later, as Lord Eccles, Minister for the Arts, he came to speak in my series of St Lawrence Jewry lunchtime talks.) On completion, it was rededicated by the Archbishop of Canterbury, Dr Geoffrey Fisher, in the presence of HM The Queen Mother. The College put me up for the award of the OBE. They also made me a Life Honorary

Graces on Some Shipwrights' Company Occasions

member of the Mess, an honour that I frequently exercise now that we have returned to live in retirement just outside the College gates.

Civic Banquet, 20 October 1979
Mansion House
The Rt Hon The Lord Mayor, Guest of Honour
Hobart H de C Moore, Prime Warden Locum Tenens

GRACE

It's the Shipwrights their Ladies and guests now O Lord
Whom the Lord Mayor here welcome with his warmest accord
Our reigning Prime Warden alas we're without
Whose brief sickness has caused this quick turn about
With the Immediate Past now taking the chair
The job for which he showed such a natural flair
We'll carry on much as it's ever been
Enjoying our tasty victuals in their Mayoral scene.

Amen

Notes

Frederick A J B Everard was taken ill a short while before the dinner and had to go to hospital. I was asked to make an announcement about his impending operation and to say that the chair would be taken by Hobart H de C Moore, the Immediate Past Master. Hobart, until he became Prime Warden, had been Treasurer of the Company. He brought all the skill of the Senior Partner of Moore, Stephens & Co to transform the finances of the Company. His firm of accountants was specialist in maritime work, and his long association with shipping firms gave him the incentive. With the Clerk, Clifford H Baylis, he gave a new life to the Livery.

Livery Dinner, 17 January 1980 at Ironmongers' Hall
Guest of Honour: The Rt Hon Peter Walker MP,
  Minister of Agriculture
Prime Warden: Frederick Everard

GRACE

We offer our thanks as we sit down to dine
That Prime Warden Everard fooled the doctors last time
That he's back in his place

Graces on Some Shipwrights' Company Occasions

And commands me say Grace
Though he's brought as his guest one who knows about meats
And what the Briton should pay for the things that he eats
So between us we'll make festive our well chosen board
If you'll graciously give us your blessing, O Lord.
                                                        Amen

Civic Banquet, Mansion House 1980
Prime Warden: Dr Dennis Rebbeck

Dr Rebbeck, Chairman of Harland and Woolf 1965–7 is an Irishman of Paisley-like proportions, with an uncanny sound-alike too on occasions.

GRACE

From Shipwrights, O Lord, you suffer this doggerel
Whether we're saying Grace on caviar or even cold mackerel
It's not that we want to presume on your blessing
But there's a certain feeling that gets us while dressing
That as long as Prime Warden Rebbeck doctors the chair
We'll begin with a titter and continue with flair
Of which there'll be plenty with Paisley-like blarney
To delight us and our ladies in their fine silks and lamee.
                                                        Amen

Livery Dinner, 11 May 1984
Held in the Painted Hall by kind permission of
the Admiral President, Admiral Sir Richard Fitch KCB
Prime Warden: Jack Neary

Replying to the Toast of the evening: Admiral of the Fleet Lord Lewin of Greenwich KG KCB MV DSC MVO

GRACE

Here gathered at Greenwich, Palace, Hospital, School
Over which, as we know it, Wren once laid his rule
The Shipwrights pay tribute to Nelson's boys in blue

Graces on Some Shipwrights' Company Occasions

Who, over the ages, have kept our nation both free and true
So tonight, Lord, now in this Painted Hall
Conscious of all that makes us stand tall
We pray that the Prime Warden, the Ladies and Guests
Will find that this dinner is most specially blessed.

              Amen

Livery Dinner, March 1985, Plaisterers' Hall
Prime Warden: Richard Charvet

GRACE

We've outgrown our home and so made requests
For the biggest Hall to accommodate guests
So here, Lord, tonight it's not Plaisterers you see
But Shipwrights and genuine men of the sea
Dressed in the proper rig of the day
On whose victuals a blessing we heartily pray.

              Amen

Livery Lunch, 22 April 1985, Ironmongers' Hall
Prime Warden: Richard Charvet
Guest of Honour: The Rt Hon the Lord Mayor, Dame Mary Donaldson GBE

GRACE

We saw her here we saw her there
We saw her nearly everywhere
The year in which a Lady was first our Lord Mayor
She sailed, she ski-ed, she played the Mum
And hosted us and everyone
So now we've had the pleasure
The Freedom which we treasure
To see her offered, Shipwright made
Here in our Hall, with table laid
Bless her and us, O Lord Divine
And thy good gifts of food and wine.

              Amen

Notes

Dame Mary Donaldson, the first lady to become Lord Mayor of London, found a special place in our affections through her expertise, shared

Graces on Some Shipwrights' Company Occasions

with her husband, Sir John Donaldson, Master of the Rolls, in their love of sailing. She was made an honorary Freeman at the Court preceding the Lunch.

Installation Dinner, April 1986, Ironmongers' Hall
Prime Warden: Derek Kimber

GRACE

Hearts of oak were our ships hewn from the finest timber
And none in his day built them better than Kimber
In his honour tonight
Lord may we unite
To make his banquet the one we remember.

Amen

Notes
Derek Kimber, engineer, Naval architect, shipbuilder, has been director of Fairfields, Harland and Woolfs and chairman of Austin and Pickersgill; Sunderland Shipbuilders; Smiths Dock; Govan Shipbuilders and London and Overseas Freighters.

Livery Dinner, 19 March 1987, Glaziers' Hall
Prime Warden: Derek Kimber

GRACE

We've left our home in Glaziers' Hall to dine
On Party Ingredients food and vintage wine
We've traded Barbican for shipless Thames to view
To gaze on London Bridge, the latest still so new
And we've come to ask God's blessing
On what the Navy calls its messing
And to raise a glass to Derek Kimber too.

Amen

Notes
Party Ingredients is the excellent catering firm at Glaziers' Hall.
London Bridge. The new three span Bridge dates from 1972. It was built at a cost of £7 million out of the Bridge House Estate Fund which has accumulated great wealth since the Middle Ages. Citizens were expected to make testamentary bequests to "God and the Bridge" for the

Graces on Some Shipwrights' Company Occasions

maintenance of their many churches and the all important Bridge. John Rennie built the previous Bridge in 1831 but prior to that the first stone bridge, of some 19 spans, was started in 1176, taking 33 years to build. This is the Bridge with its shops and houses, that so often appears on painter's canvases. Records of previous wooden bridges go back to 1108 but there is evidence that the Romans first built on this same site. Rennie's bridge was bought by an American Oil Corporation and is a major tourist attraction in Lake Havasu City, Arizona. The story goes that the Americans paid £1 million, thinking they were buying the more distinctive Tower Bridge. We understand that they are very happy nonetheless with what they have got!

The Annual Banquet at Mansion House, 11 November 1987
Prime Warden: Sir Morgan Morgan-Giles

H M King Olav V of Norway was admitted to the Honorary Freedom of the Company at a Court preceding the Dinner

> GRACE
>
> Shipwrights at Mansion House with ladies attending
> Ask a blessing, O Lord, on all they're intending
> By breaking their bread in this company
> And drinking a health to His Majesty
> Alas not in rum: by splicing a mainbrace
> But in word — in this royal but doggerel Grace.
>
>   Amen

Livery Dinner, 13 January 1988, Ironmongers' Hall
Prime Warden: Sir Morgan Morgan-Giles
Guest of Honour: The Rt Hon Lord Brabazon of Tara,
    Parliamentary Under-Secretary of State,
    Department of Transport

> GRACE
>
> Shipwrights 'within the Ark Safe for ever'
> Pray that our crafts and our skills will never
> Be flooded out of our yards
> And as men of the sea
> Of the Royal and Merchant Navy

Graces on Some Shipwrights' Company Occasions

We ask — on the Queen and her ships — a blessing divine
While for those who transport our food and our wine
We give thanks, as with guests, we now sit down to dine.
Amen

Notes
On this occasion it was to the Minister of Transport that the Toast was proposed by the Hon Mr Justice Sheen who had recently reported to him in his capacity as President of the Board of Enquiry into the Zeebrugge disaster.

HMS Warrior (1860) in Portsmouth Harbour, 12 September 1991
Buffet Supper: Prime Warden: Andrew H Arnold

GRACE

Warrior was once the hub of the nation's sure shield
Our first ironclad's shells could alone victory yield
But tonight — while preserved in that bellicose glory
She tells, with a blessing, a very different story
Of welcome, hospitality and that in which the Prime Warden delights
To make this one of our most memorable nights.
Amen

HMS Warrior 1860: 'the greatest warship in the world' — 'the black snake among rabbits' — Napoleon III. She is a new and breathtaking sight in Portsmouth Habour: her four vast decks have been faithfully restored to their original glory, each vividly portraying life in the 19th century Navy. She was the first iron-hulled, iron-clad warship. Dedicated craftsmen at Hartlepool took eight years to restore her at a cost of £7,000,000.

Livery Dinner: Ironmongers' Hall, 16 January 1992
Prime Warden: Andrew H Arnold

GRACE

We've presented our awards, our honours and prizes
And welcomed our guest list with its distinguished surprises

Graces on Some Shipwrights' Company Occasions

Lord bless us all
Here mustered in Hall
Who now hunger and thirst for all the Menu advises.

                                                                  Amen

Guests included Mr Ludovic Kennedy (writer and broadcaster) and Commodore C J S Craig, CB DSC RN, Chief of Staff, Flag Officer Naval Aviation — recently commanding at sea in the Gulf operation. The Shipwrights present awards, honours and prizes each year. On this occasion, the Queen's Silver Medal was presented to Lee Irvine of Cammell Laird Shipbuilding.

Livery Dinner: Ironmongers' Hall, 5 March 1992
Prime Warden: Andrew H Arnold

GRACE

Bless our victuals, O Lord
And all now hungrily on board
We're shipshape and Bristol fashion
And well past the day of hard tack as our ration
For we've had a year with a Prime Warden gourmet
Who's given us the taste for things like crême brulée.

                                                                   Amen

Livery Dinner: Ironmongers' Hall, 8 March 1990

GRACE

As we sit down to dine
Lord bless our victuals and wine
And that new Freeman we'll be getting to know
When the inner man's fed
The Ensigns still white and the Duster red
We'll hear Sterling's line on his own P&O

                                                                   Amen

The new Freeman was Admiral Sir Julian Oswald GCB ADC, Chief of Staff and First Sea Lord.

    The Guest of Honour was Sir Jeffrey Sterling CBE, Chairman of P&O Steam Navigation Company (now Lord Sterling).

Graces on Some Shipwrights' Company Occasions

*Annual Banquet: at the Brewery Chiswell Street,
  29 October 1990*
Prime Warden: The Reverend E C B Corlett

> GRACE
> Tonight we have Mansion House fun
> In Whitbreads' spacious Porter Tun
> And the Prime Warden asks us to pray
> In a Shipwright-like way
> For a blessing on all the chef has now done.
>   Amen

It was thought that, owing to a two year pending refit, Mansion House would not be available when the booking was made.

Court Lunch at Ironmongers' Hall, 27 February 1990
Prime Warden: Michael Everard
*In honour of the 90th birthday of HM The Queen Mother
  attended by the HRH The Prince Philip,
  the Duke of Edinburgh, Permanent Master*

> GRACE
> God be praised
> As our hearts are raised
> By our youngest Liveryman the Royal Lady
> May our victuals be blessed
> And our wine at its best
> Our Permanent Master well pleased, Lord, we pray thee.
>   Amen

Ladies Livery Dinner: Mansion House, 30 October 1989
Prime Warden: Michael Everard

> GRACE
> In his 800th year we've the privileged pleasure
> Of here dining the Lord Mayor — something we treasure
> It leads us to pray
> In our Shipwright-like way
> That the evening's blessing will flow in very good
>   measure.
>   Amen

Graces on Some Shipwrights' Company Occasions

Livery Banquet: Ironmongers' Hall, 20 April 1989
Prime Warden: Michael Everard

> GRACE
>
> We're At Home to all friends of the Livery
> As we sit down in our Hall now to dine
> With a guest — almost one of the family —
> Through him who loved cigars, whisky and wine
> So Lord we pray
> In a Shipwright-like way
> For a blessing on all whom we hail 'Ahoy'
> And on all the goodies we're about to enjoy.
>
>   Amen

Note
The Prime Warden's principal guest was Winston Churchill MP, grandson of 'a former Naval person'.

The Annual Banquet: The Mansion House,
Monday 31 October 1988
Prime Warden: Graham R Newman

> GRACE
>
> Before we raise our knives and forks
> And enjoy what comes from well drawn corks
> We Shipwrights and men of the sea
> Of the Royal and the Merchant Navy
> Ask a blessing divine
> Not just on Mansion House goodies and glasses of wine
> But on our guests and the lovelies who now with us dine.
>
>   Amen

Supper after the annual Thanksgiving Service
Butchers' Hall: 16 May 1991
Prime Warden: Andrew H Arnold

> GRACE
>
> 'That they may return in safety to enjoy the blessings of the land
> With the fruits of their labours', is the prayer that we make:

Graces on Some Shipwrights' Company Occasions

    That we and our shipmates will always be grateful for
        what we partake.

Amen

Naval forces were at the time deployed in the Gulf.

COURT LUNCHES: TRINITY HOUSE

Each year lunch is given by the Court to honour the wife of the past Prime Warden on whom the honorary Freedom of the Company is conferred at the preceding Court meeting.

TRINITY HOUSE

The Corporation of Trinity House is an unique maritime organisation which throughout its long and distinguished history has had, as its prime objective the safety of shipping and the welfare of sailors. A Charter of 1514 gave it general powers to regulate pilotage and, in 1604, James I conferred on it rights concerning the compulsory pilotage of shipping, and the exclusive right to license Pilots in the River Thames. Its headquarters are in an impressive Georgian building in Trinity Square on Tower Hill. The Dining Room overlooks the Tower and the eye carries through to the River. It is just large enough to accommodate the Court and their Ladies on these very delightful summer occasions. Lunches are relaxed and comfortable, the ladies indulging somewhat in a post Ascot hat parade, adding charm to the occasion and brightening the day of our elderly Liverymen.

To honour Mrs Hobart H de C Moore, 19 July 1979

Hobart Moore's year as Prime Warden, after being honorary Treasurer of the Company for several years, is acknowledged to have been the watershed in our fortunes and status. Decorously supported by the effervescing and super efficient Brenda, they entertained generously at Thornhill where they also found time to develop a herd of pure-bred Sussex beef cattle. Family man, Chairman of the Royal Shakespeare Trust, on the Court of the City University as well as extending the family firm of Moore Stephens & Co worldwide, his premature death in 1981 robbed us all of the promise of much more to come. His wife has taken up his mantle in many ways, and confirms the wisdom of the honour which the Company did her.

Graces on Some Shipwrights' Company Occasions

GRACE

Our past Prime Warden's Lady has been honoured O Lord
With a Freedom with which we are all in accord
Her virtues and Hoby's in a year that's a fable
We celebrate now at this well laid-up table
And on all wives and sweethearts, good food and good wine
We ask for Your blessing as we sit down to dine.

Amen

Lunch following the Prime Wardenship of Frederick Everard, Widower, July 1980

It was a great pleasure to be able to use this occasion to congratulate on his promotion, and to welcome, Admiral of the Fleet, Sir Henry C Leach GCB and Lady Leach. To our great pride, he was later to be of decisive encouragement to the Falklands expedition.

GRACE

Trinity House, on these occasions, O Lord
Finds our Court assembled in happy accord
To honour a past Prime Warden's wisdom
By granting his lady her well earned Freedom
Alas, things are different, and in her place
He's asked that instead when I'm saying Grace
A blessing, I'll pray, and also beseech
Your good will on Sir Henry — and his Lady — Leach.

Lunch to honour Mrs David S Clarabut, July 1982

After distinguished War service in the Fleet Air Arm — awarded the DSC in 1944 — David Clarabut devoted his life, in various ways, to the River Thames. He was Managing Director of the Proprietors of Hays Wharf 1972. His year marked the bicentenary of the Grant of Livery and he carried out a splendid programme of events frequently accompanied by his wife.

GRACE

We're proud, Lord, to have Ironmongers as home
But annually grateful for Trinity House as a loan

Graces on Some Shipwrights' Company Occasions

When we take our ladies to lunch
And of the two we are sure where we'd far rather be
Blessed, when we're honouring the beautiful Clarabut Dee.

Amen

Lunch to honour Lady Charles Alexander, July 1984

The Alexanders live in a most delightful but remote part of Kent. I am a fairly frequent weekend visitor and the approach road can seem never ending. They have problems of transport. Anne has certainly had her problems, like other wives, of fetching and carrying and continuing to be at the right place at the right time.

> GRACE
>
> The wives of Prime Wardens their Freedom are given
> For in the year of his office they've toiled and miles driven
> As has Anne, with her Charles deep in Kent
> Where I tangled with shears once when I went
> Lord bless them both
> And these goodies with which the kitchens have striven.
>
> Amen

Lunch to honour Mrs Jack Neary, July 1985

In quick succession, Jack was President of the City Livery Club: the United Wards Club: the Shipwrights and then he was Sheriff. These occasions, with the required long frocks and hair do's, can take their toll of the Ladies when three, four or five nights a week finds them on duty. Cathie always came up sparkling.

> GRACE
>
> There was nothing, O Lord, remotely dreary
> In the year that you gave us Prime Warden Jack Neary
> He wined us: he dined us
> And fulfilled all our hopes
> On coming out top in the Shrieval votes
> But he could not have done it, not even he
> Without the wonderful help of the lovely Cathie.
>
> Amen

Graces on Some Shipwrights' Company Occasions

Lunch following the Prime Wardenship of Richard C L Charvet, July 1986

It was an occasion when the Freedom was bestowed on both the Admiral and Lady Staveley. The Admiral had just been appointed First Sea Lord and Chief of Naval Staff.

> GRACE
>
> We've polished up our Freedom and bestowed it carefully
> On Admiral Sir William and Lady Staveley
> 'Up spirits' we can say
> And a blessing too we pray
> On our victuals, tots and all the boys at sea
> But especially for the Ruler of the Queen's Navy.
>
>   Amen

Lunch to honour Mrs Derek Kimber, July 1986

> GRACE
>
> In the course of his year Past Prime Warden Kimber
> Proved himself hewn from the best sort of timber
> But at Trinity House on our Court Ladies Day
> It's our praise that we offer as Grace we now say
> And our thanks to his wife — who surpasses him, when
> She's just being the adorable, blonde, willowy Gwen.
>
>   Amen

July 1988

The Past Prime Warden, Sir Morgan and Lady — Marigold — Morgan-Giles were taking part in a race at sea and were unable to be present on this traditional occasion at Trinity House.

> GRACE
>
> Marigold today, she's a sailor at sea
> But we know where she'd otherwise be
> We can still, then, say Grace
> In our favourite place
> Beloved by all maritime men
> — Thanks be,
>
>   Amen

Graces on Some Shipwrights' Company Occasions

The Court Ladies Lunch, July 1989
Watermen's and Lightermen's Hall

GRACE

Watermen and Lightermen welcome us today
With Doggetts Coat and Badge on such colourful display
But even so that splendour does not readily compare
With what our Shipwrights' Ladies so elegantly wear
We thank you Lord for all of them and the good things we'll enjoy
Specially for the Freeman, youngest and most talented, the incomparable Joy.

Amen

Lunch was held at the Watermen's and Lightermen's Hall as Trinity House was being refurbished. The dining hall at Watermen's had also just been elegantly enlarged to include a display cupboard of colourful Watermen's uniforms.

At Trinity House (newly refurbished) 19 July 1990

GRACE

It's good to be back where we think we belong
With its refurbished decor — for 'we few' not the throng
What better place
To offer a Grace
And a blessing on what's done for our lady Ann
The wife of none other than — Marathon Man.

Amen

The Master, F Michael Everard competed successfully in the Marathon

Ladies Lunch: Trinity House, 18 July 1991
Prime Warden: Andrew H Arnold

GRACE

All seafarers have as their patron St Andrew
His Christian namesake Prime Wardens this happy crew
He's generously seen to our tots
Now on our luncheon flesh-pots
Asks a blessing — to add to our thanks
To Ewan and Edna, the couple from Manx.

Amen

Graces on Some Spectacle Makers' Company Occasions

Past Prime Warden and his wife, Ewan and Edna Corlett, live in the Isle of Man. It was also the first occasion on which Ewan wore his clerical collar after ordination on St Peter's Day. He was awarded a doctorate in Naval architecture by Durham University. He is a world famous expert on ship salvage and was Honorary Architect for the reconstruction of S S *Great Britain*.

Livery Dinner: The Painted Hall, Greenwich, 8 May 1992
Installation of Prime Warden: D I Moor

GRACE

Ave atque vale
Hail to the new: our historian who's become our Prime Warden
Farewell to the Old(ing): our clerk of whom opinions are golden
Lord bless them both and all
Here in the Painted Hall
Who to your bounty are thankfully beholden.
                                        Amen

David Ian Moor became a Liveryman of the Company by redemption. He is Honorary Historian and author of the book on the Company's treasures. He is a chartered engineer and naval architect specialising since 1947 in the hydrodynamic design of large ships. I had the pleasure of marrying his Liveryman son, James, to Annette Faith Walker, a former accountant with Ellerman Lines and herself a Liveryman. It is an unique case of two Liverymen of the Company marrying.

Robert Olding retired as Clerk after 5 years of strenuous and devoted service. Strangely, he had come to us after a distinguished career in the Royal Air Force. He was a Group Captain with a CBE and DSC.

THE WORSHIPFUL COMPANY OF SPECTACLE MAKERS
Charter: 16 May 1629
Order of precedence: 60

The Company is the best evidence of the importance of the Freedom to 17th century traders. Only when they were made free of the City by the

Graces on Some Spectacle Makers' Company Occasions

Charter of 1629 were Spectacle Makers (Freemen up till then of the Brewers' Company) able to practise and regulate the mystery of their own craft. To a remarkable extent this is still the case as the Company is an examining body with a professional interest in continuing education and refresher courses for both opthalmic and dispensing opticians. As testimony to this role, there are over 4000 Freemen (and women) whereas the Livery, granted in 1809, is limited to 200. This involvement with their trade is paralleled in the Goldsmiths continuing to hallmark all articles of gold, silver and platinum: the Fishmongers inspecting fish sold in the London market and the Gunsmiths 'proving' all hand guns and marking them 'lock, stock and barrel'. Their original Charter is in pristine condition. It has survived fires and other hazards of City life, and is set out on two skins of vellum with a large wax impression of the Privy Seal affixed by its original cord.

They have no Hall of their own. How well they did in 1946 in becoming tenants of the Apothecaries! Their Hall in Blackfriars Lane, built shortly after the Great Fire, was scarcely affected by the War. It has the authentic feel of the 17th century about its panelled walls and imposing staircase.

There is an integrity about this Company's historic roots and continuing purpose which makes it of special interest. I delight in having been presented with its Freedom and Livery and warmly echo the traditional toast given by the Clerk at the end of every banquet:

> 'The Master, Wardens and Fellowshippe of Spectacle Makers of London; may they flourish — root and branch — for ever!'

Livery Dinner at Apothecaries' Hall, 1985
Master: Sir Richard Meyjes

GRACE

Spectacle Makers have foregathered in Apothecaries' Hall
To the great delight and joy of each and all
And Sir Richard Meyjes further requests
For the Lord Mayor, his Lady and all of his guests
That you'll bless the silver and glass, O Lord
And all we have eyes to see at his Masterly board.

                                                     Amen

Graces on Some Spectacle Makers' Company Occasions

Sir Richard Meyjes, like all Masters of this Company, served for two years: 1985–7. After distinguished War service in India, the Middle East and Europe, he qualified as a solicitor and spent most of his life in the legal department of Shell International. He has been Deputy Lieutenant and High Sheriff of Surrey and Chairman of the Council of the University of Surrey.

Livery Ladies Banquet at Mansion House, 10 June 1987
Master: Sir Richard Meyjes

GRACE

On the eve of the battle of Polling Day
Spectacle makers gather in splendid array
With ladies as lovely as this Mansion House Hall
Away from nightly broadcasts that have held us in thrall
We'll seek now your blessing O Lord Divine
On us and your gifts of good food and wine.

Amen

Livery Dinner at Apothecaries' Hall, 18 July 1987
Master: Professor H J A Dartnall

GRACE

We're hosting the Lord Mayor in the Hall of
    Apothecaries'
Than which, for its history surely better there none is
So giving thanks for our tenancy of this special venue
And ere with our spectacles reading this menu
We pray, Lord that though eyes may be distended by
    wine
You'll keep us mindful of driving, yet bless all who dine.

Amen

GRANT OF LIVERY BY PRESENTATION

'It is extremely rare that a grant of the Livery by presentation is made — indeed it is the highest honour that the Company can bestow.'

The Charge to a new Liveryman
(taken from the original Ordinances of the Company, 1630)
'You shall be true to our Sovereign Lady the Queen her Heirs and Successors and you shall perform and obey all that to you appertaineth

Graces on Some Spectacle Makers' Company Occasions

to be done by the true meaning of the Book of Ordinances of this Society being honest for you to perform and approved or warranted by the Laws of the Realm.'

From the Company magazine
At a meeting of the Court in Apothecaries' Hall on Thursday 24 November, 1990, our Chaplain the Reverend Basil Watson was clothed as of the Livery after taking the appropriate oath of allegiance. Basil Watson, who served for many years as a Chaplain with the Navy, now has his home at Greenwich after serving as the vicar of St Lawrence Jewry next Guildhall until his retirement. He was also Rural Dean of the City and he has served as Chaplain to the Spectacle Makers' Company since 1981.

Always ready to do all he can to assist our Company, he has a considerable ability to stop us in our tracks and make us think afresh on matters of practical and current importance. His belief in the relevance of Christian principles to everyday life is both infectious and challenging and we are very pleased to welcome him to the Livery.

Needless to say, he was not short of an appropriate grace at the lunch which followed his admission:

    GRACE

    Before Spectacle Makers take wine
    They ask for a blessing divine
    On all they're about to enjoy
    It's their youngest Liveryman too
    Of whom they've kindly made much ado
    Who now raises his voice
    So you hear him rejoice
    And pledge to be loyal and true.
                                                    Amen

By courtesy of Richard Thorpe, Editor of the Company's magazine.

Livery Dinner at Mansion House, 3 June 1991

    GRACE

    Special blessings we ask, Lord, as we sit down tonight
    On all the goodness with which our table's bedight
    For we're almost the last to be here at all
    While a Lord Mayor resides in this baronial hall

Graces on Some Carmens' Company Occasions

> Even more specially, as our Livery have asked her
> We celebrate the fabulous Anne Silk as our first Lady Master.
>
> Amen

The builders moved in during the following month to begin a two-year refurbishment of the Mansion House.

Mrs Anne Arnold Silk was the first Lady Master on the Company's Roll: she was among the first ladies of any Livery Company to be its Master.

Livery Dinner at Apothecaries' Hall, Wednesday 3 June 1992
Master: James L Kennerley Banks

GRACE

> In Press and Media we see him daily here and there
> Our City harbinger, ubiquitous Lord Mayor
> We're honoured that tonight with us he dines
> To savour and enjoy our fine well-tasted wines
> O Lord, who thyself did sit at meat with saint and sinner
> Be present now to bless this special Livery Dinner.
>
> Amen

Note

The Lord Mayor, who attended with the Sheriffs, has hardly been off the pages of the Press since he appeared almost immediately among the rubble of the Baltic Exchange following the IRA terrorist attack. In happier mood, in the week prior to this dinner, he had been photographed in full control of a Penny Farthing cycle, promoting the City Cycle Challenge, a 50-mile charity cycle ride to Southend-on-Sea.

'Well-tasted wines': following the Charter Day Service and before Dinner, we were invited to a Wine Tasting in the Hall, hosted by Prospero Wines, from which some wines were chosen for this occasion.

THE WORSHIPFUL COMPANY OF CARMEN
Charter granted 26 June 1946 by HM The King (George VI)
Order of precedence: 77

The post World War II grant of Charter gives the erroneous impression of a Company of motoring enthusiasts and buffs of the technical details of the internal combustion engine. There are such Liverymen, but they belong to a trade first regulated in 1277: 'no cart serving the City,

Graces on Some Chartered Surveyors' Company Occasions

bringing water, wood, stones, etc. be shod with iron'. In 1485, all carts were ordered to be shod with flat nails to avoid damage to the streets. The delay of 700 years in obtaining their Charter was due mostly to vested interests, notably those of the Woodmongers. They were a powerful body, sometimes known as Fuellers (vide Company 95) as they were responsible for the carriage of wood and, later, coal, vital items in the life of the City. They exercised control until 1582 when the City, tired of the in-fighting, made Christ's Hospital responsible for regulating the Carmen and collecting their rents and fines for the benefit of the school.

Most of the problems of our sophisticated transport were experienced by the Carmen from earliest days. Carts were branded (licence plates) for purposes of identification. Streetkeepers (traffic wardens) were appointed. One-way traffic systems were established. 'Car-room' (taxi ranks) was designated and rented and 'turnkeeping' introduced — first come first served from the head of the queue.

'Plus ça change' . . . . it is not surprising that, with the importance of modern transport, the Company has provided no less than six Lord Mayors of London in recent years.

Court Luncheon at Haberdashers' Hall, 29 January 1992
Master: K E Parry

GRACE

The Court has hungered all morning, O Lord, for the sake of its Liverymen
And thirsted — within the limits of being good car (driving) men
They uphold the code
And deserve a far better ode
Than I offer as Grace — but I pray for an approving
AMEN.

                                                    Amen

THE WORSHIPFUL COMPANY OF CHARTERED SURVEYORS
Order of precedence: 85

This was the first Company formed from members of Institutes who wished to accept Livery status. It was the wish of the Aldermen, when the City was under attack in the 1970s, in the days of the Wilson

Graces on Some Chartered Surveyors' Company Occasions

Inquiry, that members of the profession would identify themselves with the Livery and give their contemporary support to what was in danger of being dismissed as an expression of archaism.

Chartered Accountants, Chartered Secretaries and Administrators and members of the Actuarial and Insurance Institutes quickly followed the Chartered Surveyors. All have added significantly to the living tradition of the City.

Livery Lunch, 1982
Master: David Male

GRACE

Good Lord bless us all
The Male of the species, as Master
With Chris, our late Clerk, who with laughter
Have both done things well
And whose praises we'll tell
When we've partaken of what follows hereafter.

                                               Amen

David Male is a Senior Partner of Gardiner & Theobald. Christian Bryant was a partner of Daniel Smith, Briant & Done. His work has included appointments as Land Steward of the Manor of Kennington of the Duchy of Cornwall and agent for All Souls College, Oxford. He is a Church Commissioner and a Governor of the Polytechnic of the South Bank. He was Clerk of the Company 1979–1982. He is a man of unfailing cheerfulness with an infectious laugh. This Grace was said at his farewell lunch.

Livery Ladies Banquet at Mansion House, 1985
Master: Richard Luff

GRACE

When Chartered Surveyors ask their guests here to dine
On their very good food and perhaps better wine
When the Lord Mayor is guested by Dick Luff, the Master
Its the best of our evenings for music and laughter
At least I've always found it so. Benedicamus Domino.

                                               Amen

Richard Luff was very much part of the City life: City Surveyor at one time; President of the Royal Institution; Director of Property, British

Graces on Some Chartered Surveyors' Company Occasions

Telecom, which among other things, gave him an office in that fascinating BT House, looking out over, and close to, the dome of St Paul's.

Ladies Banquet at Carpenters' Hall
Master: Maxwell Taylor

GRACE

'A loaf of bread' the Walrus said
Is what we chiefly need
Peppers and vinegar besides
Are very good indeed
Pray, bounteous Lord, provide much more
And bless what caterers have in store
Smoked salmon or oysters is most agreeable to all
Chartered Surveyors who now dine in Carpenters' Hall.
Deo Gratias.

                                                                  Amen

Mansion House, 23 June 1988
Master: S K Knowles

GRACE

Chartered Surveyors, on the eve of Midsummer Day
No madness display
In bringing their ladies to dine
One may safely say
It's good sense to pray
A blessing — not least on the wine.
Deo Gratias.

                                                                   Amen

Livery Lunch at Watermen's and Lightermen's Hall
Master: S K Knowles

GRACE

In Watermen's Hall
We're all held in thrall
By Doggetts Coats and Badges —
And now Lord before Surveyors take wine

Graces on Some Chartered Surveyors' Company Occasions

They ask your blessing divine
That will repair the forenoon's ravages.

                    Amen

Livery Lunch at Pewterers' Hall

GRACE

On Budget Day
Surveyors pray
That their estates will get a fair deal
And on food and wine
A blessing divine
So, at least, we'll have a square meal!

                    Amen

Livery Lunch at Armourers' and Braziers' Hall,
30 November 1989
Master: John Trustram Eve

GRACE

God bless this bunch
As they munch their lunch
May their table talk weave
Masterly thoughts
For John Trustram Eve.

                    Amen

The Seminar Dinner at Armourers' and Braziers' Hall,
8 February 1990
Master: John Trustram Eve

GRACE

At Armourers and Braziers we dare
With J Trustram Eve in the chair
To ask that our victuals be blest
With our wine at its best
As we survey the bounteous fare
And our converse have Surveyor-like flair.

                    Amen

Graces on Some Chartered Accountants' Company Occasions

Court Luncheon at Pewterers' Hall, 19 November 1991
Master: The Hon Michael Clarke

> GRACE
>
> These familiar faces, O Lord
> Add a piquancy to this luncheon board
> It's a scene at Pewterers I've often surveyed
> And my best graces not infrequently prayed
> As Michael Clarke's Livery still look a great bunch
> It's a year's blessing I ask — and a jolly good lunch.
>
> Amen

On retirement, after 12 years as their Chaplain, I was entertained to lunch and presented with a large, beautifully mounted and framed historical print of the City (1755). Circumstances had delayed this occasion by a year or more. I was sad to leave the Company.

THE WORSHIPFUL COMPANY OF
CHARTERED ACCOUNTANTS
Grant of Livery Status, 19 April 1977
Order of precedence: 86

One of six Institutes whose members were offered the Livery at the same period, the Worshipful Company of Chartered Accountants have been fortunate in being able to use the Great Hall of the Institute for their annual Installation Dinner and at certain other times. It is a magnificent Hall in Moorgate Place and has table silver worthy of its modern splendour.

Installation Court Dinner, the first Chartered Institute Hall, October 1977
Master: James Keith

> GRACE
>
> Bless, O Lord, the members of this new Livery, especially the Master, shortly to be installed, his Wardens and Court.
> Throughout its years may this Company play its part in the life of our City. Let its table be graced with 'true and fair' fellowship, good wine and good food.
>
> Amen

Graces on Some Chartered Accountants' Company Occasions

Ladies Livery Banquet at Mansion House, May 1979
Master: Alan Hardcastle

GRACE

Wearing their Livery for the first time
The Company, marooned in their jackets, have come here to dine
They've already certified sales
In England and Wales
So account them, Lord, worthy of wine.

                                                 Amen

A great innovation, yet reminiscent of the tradition of distinctive colour in each Livery, was the adoption of a maroon velvet jacket which can be worn as a dinner jacket in place of evening dress, or on other appropriate occasions.

Ladies Livery Banquet at Mansion House, May 1983
Master: Sir Kenneth Cork

GRACE

The tables are laid, they've drawn the corks
But ere we now raise our knives and our forks
Keep us mindful, O Lord, of those bathroom scales
And think kindly of Chartered Accountants in England and Wales.

                                                 Amen

Sir Kenneth Cork was Senior Partner in W H Cork Gully & Co whose office was next to the church in Guildhall House. He most kindly wished me into the Chaplaincy of the Company from its inception. Among my trophies, I treasure a fun lighter embedded in an outsize cork. It was a present which he gave to those with whom he dined in his year. He did so at Sion College while I was President.

Court Livery Dinner at National Westminster Bank, 23 January 1984
Master: Martin Harris, a director of National Westminster Bank

GRACE

O Lord bless our eating and drinking and telling of tales
And defend us from leaking those insiders' tales
And within Colonel Siefert's upstanding forum

Graces on Some Launderers' Company Occasions

Help us behave with proper decorum
As befits Chartered Accountants in England and Wales.
Amen

On my retirement, the Company most kindly presented me with a silver goblet by Alex Telford. It handles well and gets washed up in hot water much more frequently than it needs polishing! My years as their Chaplain took me to Partners' tables in all the great named Companies. I have a feeling that one of the better sermons which I preached was on the theme which acknowledged their indispensable role in the City:
Quis Custodiet ipsos Custodes?

THE WORSHIPFUL COMPANY OF LAUNDERERS
Order of precedence: 89

Livery Companies are still being formed. From the Crafts and Professions and the Service Industries, men and women, who share a common purpose, express their interest in becoming part of what is, therefore, a continuing City tradition. Since the War, 18 companies have become part of the Livery. They further the same ideals that inspired their medieval forebears: standards of craftsmanship and professionalism to be upheld: charity exercised and religious practices followed. One of these new Companies is the Launderers. I have had the good fortune to be their Chaplain for the past 20 years and have tried to encapsulate their progress to fully fledged Livery status in the various Graces composed.

My invitation to be Chaplain came through Arthur Oliver, Chairman of Chapman's Laundry in Portsmouth. He rang on seeing in *The Times* my appointment to St Lawrence Jewry. 'Please stand by to be our Chaplain. I'm Renter Warden and hope to be Master of the Launderers in due course. Come for the weekend and let's talk about it.' His generous invitation to be Chaplain was later regularised by the Court.

My wife and I spent a most delightful weekend with Arthur and Betty in their home, Pond Head, Hayling Island, the house in which Nevil Shute wrote *On the Beach*.

I had known him from my naval days when he was Vice Chairman of Portsmouth FC. His mother, Annie Oliver, was a great figure in charity work when I was successively Chairman of Aggie Weston's and the YMCA. We were much indebted to her fund raising efforts on our behalf; and the family became part of our lives. Arthur enthused me with his hopes for the new Company: an enthusiasm which has increased with the years as the Company has grown to its cherished responsibilities.

Graces on Some Launderers' Company Occasions

The Launderers were constituted by an Order of the Court of Aldermen of the City of London on 11 December 1977 and the Grant of Livery, consequent on that, was confirmed shortly afterwards by Letters Patent presented by the Lord Mayor at a ceremony in Mansion House.

Luncheon to the Court of Aldermen following the formal presentation to the Grant of Livery at Mansion House on Friday 10 March 1978
The Rt Hon the Lord Mayor Air Commodore The Hon Sir Peter Vanneck GBE, CB, AFC, AE, MA, ScD, DL

> GRACE
>
> Our table, Lord, is furnished well with guests and
> adorned with linen made clean by our craft. Bless,
> therefore, thy gifts to our use and ourselves to thy service
> and the honour of our Livery now granted us by this City.
>
> Amen

That occasion represented the fulfilment of an ambition of a group of Launderers who first met informally in 1955 and held their inaugural meeting on 23 February 1960. During those sometimes long 12 years of apprenticeship, they were recognised as a City Company (without a grant of Livery) with an approved Constitution and Ordinances. By that, they became entitled to be called a Worshipful Company. As guardians of civic life, the Court of Aldermen require the fulfilment of certain standards and obligations before the full Grant of Livery, not least the building up of a charitable fund in excess of £100,000. That all took time which, in the event, has made the Company more rightly proud of its hard-earned status.

Lunch to mark the Silver Anniversary held at Launderers' Hall.
Monday 25 February 1985
Master: Jack Pennell, 1984–5
Most of the Founding members were present

> GRACE
>
> Time was, Lord, when the Aldermen's Court looked like
>   an adversary
> But, by your Grace, its delays proved salutary
> For our iron was roused
> And our dolly got housed

Graces on Some Launderers' Company Occasions

Where we now proudly stand
With our founders so grand
On this Silver Anniversary.

                                                          Amen

The Iron and the Dolly are, with the Cat, our emblems. They are incorporated in the Arms granted by the College of Heralds in 1963. Subscribed is our motto 'Cleanliness is next to Godliness'. The shield, bearing this device, took its place in 1980 in sequence alongside the previous 88 other shields, all secured in the ceiling of Guildhall.

Traditional, too, is the March of the Master Launderers. Played as the chief guests in procession take their places, it is a medley of tunes associated with the 19th century industry: 'Dashing away with a smoothing iron' and 'The Irish Washer-woman' among them.

I use 'our' as the Company very kindly made me an honorary Liveryman, together with Sir Hugh Wontner (Chairman of the Savoy, with its extensive laundry) and Sir David Rowe Ham, our sponsoring Alderman.

Finding a home for 150 Liverymen in the space-starved City presented many problems. Fortunately, through a magnificent response from the Livery and from the Industry, money was raised to buy a one third share (with the Glaziers and Scientific Instrument Makers) in a listed warehouse building on the South Bank waterfront alongside London Bridge and within a short processional distance of Southwark Cathedral, our place of worship.

From the River Room of this Launderers' Hall, so called whenever it is being used by the Company, there is a view of Fishmongers' Hall across the Thames and, indeed, a panorama of all the City that is second to none. It is a view that is especially scenic when floodlit. We benefit greatly when we foregather for dinner. For this imaginative purchase, the Company is greatly indebted to the tireless interest of W J Marle during his time as Renter Warden (1978-9).

Ladies Banquet, Friday 18 May 1984
The Lord Mayor of London Dame Mary Donaldson GBE
   attending in the Borough of Southwark
Master: Stuart Laurie-Walker

    GRACE

    From Southwark whence our City is most beautifully seen

Graces on Some Launderers' Company Occasions

We Launderers rejoice in our home and its napiery clean
So Lord bless our food and wine
As with ladies and guests we sit down to dine
Because among them we're honoured, as in a dream
By the Lord Mayor of London and the whole civic team.

              Amen

The first Livery Dinner following the entry to Launderers' Hall by the Company, Monday 18 October 1982
Master: Richard Seaman

GRACE

We've laundered, O Lord, we've starched and we've pressed
Enabling our City to be decently dressed
For our Livery we've laboured: for years we've been tried
But now we've a home in which we take pride
It's our thanks then that we offer as well as request
That our hall and our board may always be blessed.

              Amen

Ladies Banquet, Wednesday 18 May 1983
Guest of Honour: HRH The Princess Royal
Master: Richard Seaman

GRACE

It's our home, Lord, where we're dining tonight
To honour our guests, and hopefully delight
HRH with our craft and our dressing
Our shirts starched and ironed and whiter than white
Our napkins, fair linen, all pressed till they're right
All we ask, good Lord, now — is your blessing.

              Amen

Livery Dinner at Tallow Chandlers' Hall,
Monday 16 October 1978
Master 1978–9: Brian W Goodliffe (Chairman Smarts Laundry)

GRACE

Brian Goodliffe, O Lord, is the Master
Who presides at our table tonight

Graces on Some Launderers' Company Occasions

And prays that you send us a blessing
On all gifts that await our delight
Well laundered are napkins and placemats
They bring pride and joy to our hearts
There's but one thing professionally we question
Could anyone have done it better than Smarts?

                                                          Amen

Ladies Night Banquet at Tallow Chandlers' Hall, May 1979
Master: Peter MacDonald

GRACE

We've all had our champers, our sherry, our gin
Before we were bidden our meat to begin
So we Launderers, O Lord,
At our well fullered board
Beg your blessing as we sit down to dine
On this promising menu and good vintage wine
And not least on our Ladies and their happy laughter
But on Peter MacDonald our most excellent Master.

                                                          Amen

Livery Dinner following the Annual Livery Service in
    Southwark Cathedral, 14 October 1985
Master: Roy le Poidevin

GRACE

We've been singing in Church and confessing our sin
And Launderers now ask a blessing ere we begin
To wine and to dine
All fullered and fine
And ever mindful of stories of kith and of kin
And intrigued by the name of our Roy le Poidevin.

                                                          Amen

Graces on Some Launderers' Company Occasions

Ladies Night Banquet, 22 May 1987
Guests of Honour: The Most Revd and Rt Hon The Lord Archbishop of Canterbury, Dr Robert Runcie (hereafter — 'The Good');
The Rt Hon The Lord Mayor of London,
Sir David Rowe-Ham (Hon Liveryman, 'The Great')
Master: Derek Hirst

GRACE

Launderers here welcome the Great and the Good
To partake, when its blessed, of our wine and our food
We're spick too and span and whiter than white
As befits us for ladies on this special night
But it's Grace that comes first
So, Lord, bless us all
In our Livery Hall
Especially the Master, our own Derek Hirst.

Amen

Livery Dinner, Monday 12 October 1987
Toast to the Company proposed by Sir Alex Jarratt Chancellor of Birmingham University
Master: William H Davidson MBE

GRACE

Before we raise our knives and forks
And enjoy what comes from well drawn corks
Or welcome guests: Alex Jarratt and all
To the well fullered tables of Launderers' Hall
Or hear great talk of what's laid on
For the Masterly year of Bill Davidson
Lets bless and praise our Lord divine
For his good gifts of food and wine.

Amen

Graces on Some Launderers' Company Occasions

Livery Dinner at Launderers' Hall, Tuesday 17 May 1988
Guest of Honour: The Rt Hon The Lord Mayor of London,
  Alderman Sir Greville Spratt GBE
Master: William H Davidson

> GRACE
>
> Jack Sprat could eat no fat
> His wife could eat no lean
> And so between them both, you see
> They licked the platter clean
> And it's cleanliness, of course, dear Lord
> That Launderers always say
> Should be the feature of our board
> When Lord Mayors make our day.
>
>   Amen

An occasion when Gordon Jones proposed a toast to the guests among whom he included me:

> Basil Watson our Chaplain supreme
> Has a wit more than sharp — razor keen
> Every time that we dine
> There's a Grace that's in rhyme
> And, of course — just for us — it's quite clean.

The 'classical' Grace which others accuse me of using on all Launderers' occasions!

> OMO LUX DOMESTOS BROBAT

Ladies Banquet at Launderers' Hall, 17 April 1989

> GRACE
>
> On Lady's Day
> All Launderers pray
> For the cleanliness that keeps them next to their
>   Maker
> And also ask
> On their victuals and wine
> A blessing divine
> To approve the Masterly good taste of John Baker.
>
>   Amen

Graces on Some Launderers' Company Occasions

Livery Dinner after Annual Service in Southwark Cathedral Monday 15 October 1990

GRACE

We always honour cleanliness
And are still athirst for godliness
So Lord, graciously bless us all
As we stand clean within and without in Launderers' Hall
That Party Ingredients may have just what
Meets the Masterly approval of our Freddie Scott.

                                                          Amen

Ladies Banquet at Launderers' Hall, 5 April 1991

GRACE

What fun it is Lord when we Launderers dine
Fed by Party Ingredients on good food and fine wine
Tonight it's even more so as the Master's Grace now requests
With the Lord Mayor, wives and sweethearts as our special guests
How lovely they look in this our own Hall
I've to confess, as a bonus, that I love 'em all.

                                                           Amen

Dinner after the Annual Service in Southwark Cathedral at Launderers' Hall
14 October 1991
Master: J Anthony Dunn

GRACE

Deo Gratias
'I must go down to the seas again, to the lonely sea and the sky
And all I ask is a tall ship and a star to steer her by':
So mused the Master on his yacht in the Med
As he took a long sight on tonight's board and bed
But in upping that anchor surely a blessing he's won
And we'll not know him now as Tony but as J Duty Dunn.

                                                           Amen

Graces on Some Insurers' Company Occasions

J Anthony Dunn is a keen yachtsman: he had appropriately sailed on his Election Day from the east coast with Past Master Michael Ross and Court Assistant Michael Bennett, to St Katherine's Dock, Tower Bridge. His Guest at Dinner was the Rt Hon The Lord Burnham, Chairman of the Sail Training Association. The Lesson which he read at the Cathedral service, was from Acts Chapter 27: the story of St Paul in the storm-tossed sea that led to the shipwreck at Malta.

Ladies Banquet at Launderers' Hall, 1st May 1992
Master: J Anthony Dunn

GRACE

White tie and tails — our romantic night's now begun
Our napkins are well fullered and perfectly done
We too are all laundered and look at our best
Our ladies and guests hopefully are duly impressed.
So, please Lord, bless our evening that should be such fun
And bring pride to our Master — J Anthony Dunn.

Amen

THE WORSHIPFUL COMPANY OF INSURERS
Order of precedence: 92
The Insurers' Hall, 20 Aldermanbury, EC2

The Company is fortunate in being able to use the premises built in 1957 by the Chartered Insurers' Institute. In 1983, when J A S Neave was both President of the Institute and Senior Warden, the Company was able to help with major alterations which have provided it with a distinguished Livery Hall.

1979 was the year of receiving both a Charter of Incorporation and Livery status by grant of Letters Patent. It was fitting that, at this time, Sir Kenneth Cork was Lord Mayor. As an Alderman, he had championed the idea of offering Livery status to members of the long established Institutes of various professions. The advent of such a company in his year added considerable impetus to the post-war move to free the Livery from the charge of archaism and identify it with the professional activities which help to make the City one of the busiest financial capitals of the 20th century.

Graces on Some Fuellers' Company Occasions

Livery Ladies Banquet at Mansion House, 19 October 1979
Master: W C (Bill) Harris

GRACE

It's the Insurers, O Lord, who are here to dine
At Mansion House, privileged, for the first time
So it's your blessing we ask
While in splendour we bask
And pray that the Master, the ladies and guests
Will find that this evening is most happily blest.

Amen

Livery Ladies Banquet at Mansion House, October 1981
Master: David Palmer

GRACE

'Take no thought for the morrow'
Not words that Insurers hold dear
Except at their Mansion House banquet
On this special night of the year
When in white tie and tails
Happy humour prevails
And, we're blessed, dear Lord, here
With the very best of good cheer.

Amen

THE WORSHIPFUL COMPANY OF FUELLERS
Order of precedence: 95
Letters Patent granted 19 November 1984

Though a most recently formed Company for those involved in the Coal Industry, it had an origin, along with the Carmen, in distributing coal brought from Newcastle.

Livery Lunch at Butchers' Hall, October 1985
Master: Peter Brewis

GRACE

It's the first time that Fuellers have sat down to dine
And to share as a Livery the fruit of the vine

Graces on Some Fuellers' Company Occasions

They've acquired all that the City can yield
Including in Guildhall the Company's shield
So for all of his guests
Peter Brewis requests
A grace — and a prayer
That you'll all conserve fuel with the greatest of care.

Amen

It was through the Company that, at the time of the Miners' Strike, I met Mr (now Sir) Ian MacGregor. He promised to speak in a series of talks from my Wednesday Rostrum at St Lawrence Jewry. On the Friday before speaking, he rang to say that if the media, who were following him everywhere, showed him leaving for the States, I was not to get worried: he would be back in time: his speech was prepared. That was most thoughtful and courteous to say the least. However, in his absence, ACAS had arranged a meeting for him with the miners for Wednesday morning, and clearly he could not decline to attend. 'But I see from your handbill on this Series of Talks, that your course ends in a fortnight's time. My diary is free on the following Wednesday if you would still like me to come.' He did! So did a church so full as to make it necessary to close the outer doors.

Livery Lunch at Cutlers' Hall, June 1986

GRACE

Fuellers are lunching in Cutlers' Hall
And Arthur R Puttock, to the grief of us all
Is retiring from his office of Clerk
But he's given us such goodies to eat
Which, when blessed, and we've taken our seat
Will flavour our memories with his special mark.

Amen

Installation Dinner at Middle Temple Hall, 2 October 1990
Master: Anthony Cripps

GRACE

We've our new Master, Anthony Cripps, to install
Of all privileged places in this legally historic Hall
We're favoured and graced by our ladies as well
There's no need for me on a prayer to dwell

Graces on Some Lightmongers' Company Occasions

For we know as we sit down to dine
We're asking the good Lord to bless our meat and our wine.

Amen

Installation Lunch at Cutlers' Hall, 10 October 1991

GRACE

The Cutlers' own knives, forks and spoons we're privileged to use
Valiant trenchermen they'll prove us to be, so I muse
But on our Special Day
It's a Fuellers' blessing we pray
Not just on the spanners but on all the fun
We'll be having in the Master's year just begun.

Amen

THE WORSHIPFUL COMPANY OF LIGHTMONGERS
Order of precedence: 96

Late at night, driving back over Blackfriars, Southwark or London Bridge was an experience that always quickened the heart beat. One came over the murky Thames which acted as a dark proscenium to a Square Mile ablaze with light. Great office blocks, still lit up, stirred the imagination to immediate thoughts of that worldwide traffic in Invisibles which keeps the City involved during all twenty four hours of the day and night. St Paul's, on the perimeter skyline, with its subtly lit dome, broods over it all, like a hen with wings outstretched over its chicks, giving a meaning to this City set on a hill for those who have eyes to see. 'What a stupendous place to live' I would say, or something equally inadequate to the emotion that always swept over me. Live there we did too: 'over the shop'.

We had the most elegant of Vicarages, a four bedroomed flat. Our drawing room had Wren windows which were frames for the floodlit Guildhall. That formed a perfect theatrical backdrop which was too good ever to have drawn curtains obscuring it. Atop it all too was an unique roof garden. By courtesy of Trollope & Colls, some three tons of soil were delivered there while their tower crane was working on the construction of the west wing of Guildhall. One of the churchwardens who knew about these things, Sir Robert Bellinger, asked one day what

Graces on Some Lightmongers' Company Occasions

Vic (now Lord) Matthews (Trollope & Colls) was paying for over-sailing rights. I made it my business shortly afterwards to get the Foreman of Works to introduce me to him on the site. I called his attention to the gyrations of the jib of the crane over the church spire. 'Come on, Vicar, what do you want?' 'Soil', said I. I don't suppose that he would have argued about any sum of money that I'd asked as a contribution to church funds. Soil, on the other hand, fascinated him. 'Soil', he said, 'if you've had the roof checked out by the engineers, I'll see that you have all the skips you can take of the best top soil that I can get'. He was as good as his word. Over the years since, he has been up several times to see the rose bed: the *Mahonia japanoica* bushes: the *Cotoneaster rosaceae*: the varieties of clematis: the passion flower and a whole host of geraniums, pelagoniums and other colourful annuals to which my wife Jan gave half an hour's devotion each evening with the hose, and from which she derived great therapy. We have always delighted after Livery Dinners during the summer months in bringing people home to give them a night-cap in the garden where it was still as light as day. It was very much part of the joy for us of living in the flood-lit City. We would never have had such a garden had we depended on getting penny packets of soil up there, and were ever grateful to Lord Matthews.

Of particular delight to me, then, was an invitation from the Worshipful Company of Lightmongers, on their grant of Livery in 1984 — light is such a description of Godhead — to be their Chaplain.

Membership of the Company, as of all newly formed companies, is limited to the industry: and to 110 — the City of London DC Voltage! All sections of the lighting and electrical industry are represented: the manufacturers of lighting fittings; electrical contractors and wholesalers; lighting engineers: consultancy and lighting research engineers. When one considers that there are 15 miles of fluorescent tubing and 12,500 individual fittings and diffusers in the National Westminster Tower alone, one realises something of their contribution, and how worthy they are of being a City Livery Company. What a long way the craft, the science and the art of lighting have come from the days of their predecessors: the Tallow and the Wax Chandlers.

The shield of the Company, 96th in order of precedence, was affixed to the upper walls of Guildhall. The main feature of the shield of Arms, granted by the College of Heralds, is the emblem of the flame; and, of the Crest, the figure of the City Dragon. On its wings is set a Mill Cross in token of the part played by the late Max Millar in the inception of the

Graces on Some Lightmongers' Company Occasions

Company in 1953. The motto reads: *Dominus Illuminatio Mea Et Salus Mea* (The Lord is my Light and my Help). After the ceremony, there was a dinner for the Court held in the Old Library of Guildhall.

GRACE

Lightmongers have been hung in Guildhall
Their shield is atop the north wall
So with pride they'll now dine
But ere savouring their wine
They ask, Lord, your blessing on all.

Amen

When C C G (Rick) Foot (Director: Phillips Electrical) was Master in 1986–7, he asked if I would compose a Grace which he could use throughout the year. His parting gift to the Company was a magnificent table lectern with the Lightmongers shield on the stem and, recessed into the reading surface, two silver plates. I quote from a letter which he sent me. 'The upper plate will be machine engraved with the Grace, using a clean bold script, back filled with matt black, to ensure that it stands out well against the rest of the silver plate. An acknowledgement to you as the author will be hand engraved in a much smaller and decorative script at the bottom right of the Grace. I do feel strongly about this acknowledgement, since you have been to considerable effort to compose this Grace, which has been so well received ever since we have used it. The second plate will be located at the bottom of the reading surface to mark the occasion of its gift. Again we will use a small decorative hand engraved script. I hope that this treatment will ensure three things. First, the record of our new Grace. Second, a practical aid to speech givers for their notes. Third, an advertisement for the Lightmongers, through the display of our shield'.

Installation Dinner at Tallow Chandlers' Hall
   7 November 1987
Master: W Balmford

GRACE

Thou who art the Light of the minds that know thee
And brought sight to those who were blind
Out of darkness may we beam thy rays
To illuminate men's ways

Graces on Some Chartered Architects' Company Occasions

That now and ever
We may give thee thanks and praise.
                                                    Amen

In our correspondence, I had indicated that I regarded the first two lines as containing a separate thought about the Divine: God is Light; and that characteristic inspires our major charitable activity. Somewhat naturally, the Company supports work for the Blind, through Moorfields Eye Hospital, Guide Dogs for the Blind (our first dog is called 'Light') and research into equipment for the use of those who still live and walk in darkness. The next two lines are concerned with our profession of Lightmongering and with our moral responsibility for it as Liveryman. So we say Grace, giving thanks now (for what we are about to receive) and ever, praise.

THE WORSHIPFUL COMPANY OF CHARTERED ARCHITECTS
Order of precedence: 98

In 1984, during the 150th Anniversary of the granting of the Royal Charter by Queen Victoria to the RIBA, a number of architects decided to try to form a Livery Company to represent the profession alongside recently formed Companies representing other modern professions.

A Company was formed and was able to petition the Court of Aldermen for Livery Status which was granted on 13 September 1988. The Letters Patent confirming the grant were presented to the Master, Wardens and Court of Assistants of the Company by the Rt Hon The Lord Mayor, Sir Christopher Collett, GBE, at a ceremony in Mansion House on 21 November 1988.

Livery Dinner at Drapers' Hall, 4 April 1989

GRACE
With their Ladies
Architects dine for the first time
In full fig, at the Drapers, asking a blessing divine
On their promising victuals and good vintage wine
Their Master also further requests
For his Livery and guests
Enjoyment and fun

Graces on Some Constructors' Company Occasions

That conversation begun
Will continue to flow
Like a torrent but as smooth as his (Lord Mayor's) show.

Amen

Note 1

The Master, the late John Reid, was the inspirational designer and marshal of the Lord Mayor's Show for several years.

Note 2

The Drapers' Company is the third in order of precedence among the twelve Great Companies of the City of London. Originally, a draper was one who made woollen cloth but, as time went on, he tended to become a dealer in cloth. As the trade expanded, many auxiliary crafts were created — as weavers, fullers, spinners, carders, dyers and finishers.

The original Drapers' Hall was in St Swithin's Lane. The present site of Drapers' Hall, to which the company moved in 1541, was purchased from Henry VIII, to whom it had become forfeited on Thomas Cromwell's arrest and trial for treason.

The Hall was entirely destroyed in the Great Fire of 1666 and was rebuilt from the designs of Jarman. In 1772, after suffering considerable damage by fire, the Hall was repaired in the Adam style. It was newly fronted in 1866 and the interior was also altered, as it was again in 1898.

The Livery Hall is mainly of the Victorian and Edwardian periods. It contains portraits of British Sovereigns from William of Orange to Edward VII.

THE WORSHIPFUL COMPANY OF CONSTRUCTORS
Granted Letters Patent, 15 June 1990
Order of precedence: 99

Maxwell Caplin, a surveyor from Liverpool, conceived the idea of a new Livery Company to embrace all the disciplines involved in the building industry. He dropped in on me in the Church vestry, ostensibly to discuss his idea. 'You'll do for Chaplain', he said, as he left. I became privy to their aspirations and vicissitudes from those early days. Granting me the Freedom of their Company before they achieved Livery status was one of the honours I most proudly carried away when I left the City.

Graces on Some Constructors' Company Occasions

Strangely, there has never been a Worshipful Company of Builders, though most aspects of the industry have had their specialist companies: Masons; Tylers and Bricklayers; Joiners; Plasterers; Paviors among them. Carpenters, seniority at 26, have always been regarded as the mother company, their title as a generic term. It was felt that 'Builders' might encroach on this ancient tradition and the point was taken. After much debate, leading to a thorough reappraisal of their purpose, the Livery Consultative Committee agreed to the title of Constructors. It seemed to me to be a good distinction without a vital difference. The company should flourish.

Company Dinner at Goldsmiths' Hall, 18 July 1979
Guest of Honour: HRH The Duke of Gloucester
Master: Brian Scruby

> GRACE
>
> By courtesy of the Goldsmiths, O Lord, its the Builders this time
> Who here with Royalty are privileged to dine
> And we're asking your blessing in this gracious venue
> On the gastronomic delights of this promising menu
> And we pray that the Master and all of his guests
> Will find that this evening is most happily blest.
>
>   Amen

During the dinner, the Master, Brian Scruby, sent me a note to say that HRH enjoyed the Grace and that if I would see him afterwards he would trade one for one. 'One good Grace deserves another' said HRH. 'It may sound a bit scurrilous, but it is a good Scots Presbyterian Grace. You may be able to use it.' I have often (*vide* Old Bailey)

> Good food: Good meet: Good God — Let's eat.

Company Dinner at Tallow Chandlers' Hall, 13 March 1984
Master: Ron Taylor

> GRACE
>
> We thought at one time we'd be Builders
> But we're Constructors, and if that bewilders
> It's no disaster
> With Roy Taylor as Master
> And your blessing, good Lord, as we sit down to dine
> Will keep us all friends while biding our time.
>
>   Amen

Graces on Some Constructors' Company Occasions

Company Dinner at Tallow Chandlers' Hall, 7 March 1985
Master: Maurice Pickering

GRACE

For every glass and plateful
God make us truly grateful
And of pleasures yet to be
May we soon have Livery.

                                                            Amen

Company Dinner at Tallow Chandlers' Hall, 27 November 1986
Master: John Pryke

GRACE

From the day when our founder Max Caplin
Honoured me with a request to be Chaplain
I've doggerelled your Graces
Produced wry grimaces
But now and then trust helped entertain
But the One who is good
Has nonetheless blessed your food
And I finally pray
That He'll hasten the day
When the Aldermen are in the right mood.

                                                            Amen

Graces on Some City Livery Club Occasions

THE CITY LIVERY CLUB

All Liverymen and only Liverymen, both male and female, may join the Club. Its distinctive feature is its corporate life, never better expressed than in the annual holiday which many take together. The party usually get official recognition in the country visited, be it China, India, South America or wherever. Such groups of people get to know each other well and share their sectional interests in organised groups: Aero, Bowls, Chess, Cricket, Golf, Music, Motoring, Tennis, Yachting etc.

The Club is located in Sion College on the Victoria Embankment alongside Blackfriars Bridge. It was opened in 1886 by the Prince of Wales. Sir Arthur Blomfield was the architect. The great feature of the building is the Library containing some 90,000 books, many of which are rare and early theological works. After lunch, coffee is served there. The Club has all the usual facilities, though no bedrooms. The restaurant serves excellent lunches from 12:30–15:30 during the working week and seats rather more than a hundred.

Another feature making for the cohesion of the Club is its magazine, *The Liveryman*, a large and splendidly produced journal of the year's activities and its personalities.

Members are kept aware of their civic influence by their seemingly indestructible Honorary Secretary: Bernard L Morgan — 'Bunny' to the City. There is an annual Banquet in Guildhall and the club lunches each Lord Mayor. Many social events and visits are organised: and a Christmas lunch is a special feature.

Guildhall Banquet, 1983
President: Jack Neary

> GRACE
>
> Bless, O Lord, these gifts to our use
> And ourselves to the service of the City
> And let none of the Livery be dreary
> As in London that's of Life to be weary
> And we cannot be that
> It's like eating one's hat
> When we're provisioned by that gourmet, Jack Neary.
> Amen

Graces on Some City Livery Club Occasions

At the Tennis Section Christmas Lunch, 1987
Chairman: Bill Willson-Pemberton

GRACE

'Anyone for tennis' — was Bill's cheerful cry
'Always: summer and winter', was this section's reply
And today in this world of sport
We've the seasonal thought
Of loved ones: the needy, and those far and wide
On whom we ask a blessing, dear Lord, at this Christmastide.

                                                Amen

Dinner, Motoring Section, 15 March 1990
Chairman: Norman Collins

GRACE

It's a strange blessing we ask as we sit down to dine
For though we may want it, motorists can't have too much wine
And if we indulge in this promising meal
We're in danger of falling asleep at the wheel
So, Lord, just keep us mindful of the rules of the road
And bless the good Norman and not Mr Toad.

                                                Amen

Sion College, The City Livery Club.

THE LIVERY AND THE CORPORATION OF LONDON

The highest Office that can be voted for and held by a Liveryman is that of Sheriff.

To become Lord Mayor a Liveryman must also enter into Local Government—the Corporation of London—and be elected by the citizens as an Alderman of one of its wards.

No Liveryman can become Lord Mayor who has not been elected by his peers as a Sheriff.

The Corporation of London

The Armorial Bearings of the City of London

Arms Argent a cross gules, in the first quarter a sword in pale point upwards of the last.

Crest On a wreath argent and gules a dragon's sinister wing argent charged on the underside with a cross throughout gules.

Supporters On either side a dragon argent charged on the undersides of the wings with a cross throughout gules.

Motto "Domine Dirige Nos." *(Lord Direct Us)*

The above is a correct delineation of the Armorial Bearings of the City of London as approved by the College of Arms.

The Corporation of London

The Corporation of London is the local authority responsible for the government of the City, the Square Mile. Its function is substantially to provide the infrastructure which enables London to be one of the great financial centres of the world. Its means of doing so is through its unique Common Council, based on the Model Parliament of Edward I, presided over by the Lord Mayor, with an Alderman, elected for life (retirement at age 70 as for all Magistrates), representing each of the 25 Wards.

In addition, there are 133 Common Councilmen affectionately known as 'common scoundrels' — elected annually in December. These 'City Fathers' are proportionate in number to the electorate of the 'Rotten Boroughs', as some think of Wards with as few as 20 electors. Neat and tidy democrats, particularly those who wish to be critical of the City, regard this as anomalous. In the small and flexible City, however, always having to adapt to change and development quickly, Common Council works as well now in the post 'Big Bang' era as it has done over the centuries. (In the 12th century, Aldermen gathered a few likely men who could think of 'common' interests and they consulted with the Mayor. From 1384, councilmen were elected. In 1714, they assumed financial control and so acquired power. With some small refinements, that gave the City its present system).

The system has thrown up citizens of ability and public spirit with the skills primarily employed in the complex activity of the financial capital. They give their time and thought to the Common Council at cost to themselves: there are no attendance allowances. There is a 'free lunch' to Committee members only on occasions when Committees straddle the lunch hour. Common Councilmen are non-political and reach decisions through the exercise of conscience and rational debate in Committee, decisions which are then submitted to the three-weekly meetings of the whole Council. With experience, they go on to become Chairmen/women of Committees, looking after all aspects of the City which affect the lives of its 300,000 commuters and 6,000 residents.

The Corporation of London

Of greatest antiquity and carrying most responsibility for the Corporation's assets is the City Lands Committee. Since 1967, it has also taken over the maintenance of the City's bridges and the estates from which they are maintained. The Chairman of this City Lands and Bridge House Estates Committee is further responsible to the citizens generally, much as is the Prime Minister in another place. He/she — (Mrs Edwina Coven 1987–8) — is recognised as the Chief Commoner. The importance of the office is usually signified by the award of the CBE.

The members are served by officers and staff of a very high calibre who rejoice in such titles of antiquity as Chamberlain, Remembrancer and Comptroller, as well as Town Clerk and other offices common to local government in the rest of the country.

Committees hold annual dinners, attended by the Lord Mayor and guests who have served and helped them, and, not least, by the Minister of State with his special interest in their various activities. It is on these occasions that I have been invited to say grace.

Aldermen and their Wards

Monthly, on a Tuesday afternoon, The Lord Mayor's and the Sheriffs' large Rolls Royce limousines, streaming their pennants, come sweeping into Guildhall Yard for a meeting with the 23 other Aldermen. They meet in their Courtroom, the building that protrudes into the Yard from the west wing of Guildhall.

The motorcade represents a symbol of power and authority. It never fails to stir. For 600 years or so, their predecessors governed the City. Aldermen were men of power. They still are. Acceptance by one of the 25 Wards into which the City is divided, followed by election, confers the life-long status of Alderman (retirement is at age 70, the retiring age for magistrates, as are all Aldermen). They select the Lord Mayor from their own number each year. They give or withhold permission to join their ranks to candidates who wish to submit themselves for selection by the voters of a Ward. They tell their fellow Alderman at the end of his shrieval year whether or not they will vote for him in due course for the Mayoralty. This is an urbane procedure as it gives an Alderman three or four years to drop out of public life without stigma.

Very few are judged inadequate for the task; but there were rather more than one a year who dropped out, for health or other reasons, during my 16 years in the City. Not many citizens know that this is the average 'drop out' rate; so discreet is the procedure.

It takes 14 years or so to climb the aldermanic ladder to the Mayoralty. At a seniority of 10 or 12 years, Aldermen serve their year as Sheriff. Only Aldermen who have served that office are eligible to become Lord Mayor.

Anyone in the country who is a Freeman of the City and a Liveryman can offer himself for selection. He will have to show the colour of his money and be in a position to have time, considerable time, to give.

Aldermen are now unique to the City. In the rest of the country, the office was abolished in 1974 as it had become honorary only; being promotion for long service to the local authority and good conduct.

Aldermen and their Wards

In the City, the office has always been constitutionally structured into its government and, in this democratic age, it remains elective. Its uniqueness of treatment in 1974 was therefore not a privileged exception but a natural functional survival.

From pre-Conquest days, the City was divided into Wards, the Alderman of each being responsible for its domestic arrangements and answerable to the portreeve. The Alderman now delegates some of his current responsibility to his Deputy, usually the Senior Common Councilman of the Ward; Mr Deputy.

The Wards

Aldersgate	Cornhill
Aldgate	Cripplegate
Bassishaw	Dowgate
Billingsgate	Farringdon Within
Bishopsgate	Farringdon Without
Bread Street	Langbourn
Bridge and Bridge Without	Lime Street
Broad Street	Portsoken
Candlewick	Queenhithe
Castle Baynard	Tower
Cheap	Vintry
Coleman Street	Walbrook
Cordwainer	(25 in all)

Each Ward has its Club. Its social activities enable the Alderman to make himself known to his constituents and be better placed to serve their interests. The boundaries of Bassishaw and Cheap pass through the vestry of St Lawrence Jewry and gave me the right to belong to both Clubs, though a voter only in Cheap. I had the honour to be Chairman of each in my time. For many years, too, I was Chaplain to the United Wards Club which, since 1877, has promoted the Citizenship of London. Members have social and educational occasions and travel widely on holiday together.

They are a humanising element in City life, the basis of its personal relationships. As such, they are honoured each year by the Lord Mayor. He usually attends their annual banquet or special luncheon.

Aldermen and their Wards

Lunch Bassishaw Ward Club at Innholders' Hall
30 June 1988
Guest of honour: The Rt Hon. The Lord Mayor

> GRACE
>
> Let us ask God's blessing
> In the City
> It is a pity
> We don't dine more
> In Bassishaw
> In Gillett land where now we do
> Bless us Lord till half past two.
>
>   Amen

Lord Mayors expect lunch occasions to be over by 2.30pm. Commander Sir Robin Gillett Bt GBE RD RNR is Alderman of the Ward of Bassishaw. He was Lord Mayor 1976–7.

United Wards
Graces at the annual Mansion House Banquets

1983 President, Nick Nichols

> GRACE
>
> With our wives, our guests and high powered retinue
> We await Our Lord's blessing on this most promising menu
> For on it there's nothing of mere cheese and pickles
> But the elegant choice of President Nichols
> For when Nick and Estelle are united in thought
> They ward off the temptation to do it for naught.
>
>   Amen

1984 President, Wimburn Horlock

> GRACE
>
> Its a blessing we ask as we sit down to dine
> On this rarest of fare and the best of good wine
> And with Wimburn as host
> He'll be bound loyally to toast
> All his friendships, well seasoned by time.
>
>   Amen

Aldermen and their Wards

Wimburn was a Church Warden of SLJ and, with his wife Robin, was noted for friendships in all spheres of life. She ran Stepping Stone, the justly famed pre-prep school in Hampstead, where my grandson was immensely happy and passed confidently into Arnold House.

1985 President, R S Findlay

GRACE

Let us ask God's blessing
Having braved the snow and the ice we're now feeling fine
And ready for Grace ere we sit down to dine
With a warm welcome and toast
From Ray Findlay as host
We'll have lots of fun
As the evening's begun
But Lord, mind how we go when we're topped up with wine.

                    Amen

Weather wise, it was one of the worst nights of the year but there were no empty places.

1986 President, Peter Northall-Laurie

GRACE

There are twenty five Wards in our City
Of each there's a well known ditty
But tonight they are united
In full fig and well whited
All adding up to even more glory
For the year of our Peter and Joy Northall-Laurie.

                      Amen

Banquets at Mansion House, when ladies are present, are invariably white tie occasions.

Aldermen and their Wards

Founder's Day Banquet at Stationers' Hall, 31 October 1991
President: George K Todorvitch

GRACE

We dine as the United Wards of our City
On Founder's Day the Chairman asks for a ditty
As an expression of thanks for all that is good
Like friends of old, and well-served food
He also likes the wine to be specially bles't
For it then turns vintage — and we like that best.

                                                                              Amen

The Mayoralty

It is sometimes said that Dick Whittington was never Lord Mayor of London. Not true. When he was elected in 1416 for the third time, the office of Mayor had, two years previously, 'acquired' — it was never formally granted — the Lordship. In the City, only the Monarch takes precedence. Over the years, the Rt Hon the Lord Mayor has for certain constitutional purposes been summoned to attend the Privy Council. Otherwise, during his year in office, he rates in order of national precedence as a Cabinet Minister. He is almost automatically awarded a GBE — Knight Commander of the Most Excellent Order of the British Empire — on the day that he is presented at Westminster for the Queen's approval, following his election in the City. He is usually dubbed by the Lord Chancellor in the House of Lords. He used to be granted a Baronetcy: that ceased in 1964. Sir Edward Howard and Sir Robin Gillett, both Lord Mayors of recent years, inherited their titles from fathers who had been so honoured. They were themselves additionally awarded the GBE.

The City has had its Mayoralty since 1189. That is when the Mayor was first elected by the citizens. Prior to that, the first Citizen was the Portreeve who was the King's appointee. In a Charter of 1215, confirmed shortly afterwards by Magna Carta, the citizens of London were granted, by King John, the right annually to elect their own Mayor. It is significant that only barons were present at the signing of Magna Carta with the exception of the Mayor. Eight hundred years of Mayoralty have recently been celebrated. During those years, the office has acquired many privileges and duties which have given the City an unique status in the country, indeed, in the world. Visiting Heads of State are given a State Banquet in Guildhall on the second night of their Official Visit. Whenever the Lord Mayor travels overseas, he is recognised as an Ambassador Extraordinary and also as part of the world's folklore. Some of his many titles imply his almost daily duty and constant care: Chief Magistrate: Trustee of the fabric of St Paul's: Admiral of the Port of London: Chancellor of the City University. Duties, which were in the nature of a Chief Executive's, have, with the

The Mayoralty

progressive democratisation of civic and national life, been taken over by the Town Clerk and other local authority officers.

The Lord Mayor's role is like that of a constitutional monarch: of influence rather than power. That influence, however, given a man of real leadership calibre, can be extensive. A modern instance of the power of the Lord Mayor was the occasion on which President Ceaucescu of Romania made a State Visit to this country and, according to custom, was invited to receive an address of welcome and a banquet in his honour at Guildhall. He made it known to the Foreign Office that, as an atheist, he did not want any prayers said on formal occasions. The then Lord Mayor, Sir Peter Vanneck, informed the Foreign Office that before meetings the City Fathers repeated the City motto and that it was the custom to say Grace before City banquets. However, rather than give offence, he said that the Lord Mayor and Sheriffs would process into Guildhall as usual and Grace would be said. They would then return to the ante-room and escort the President and Mme. Ceaucescu to their places. Honour was satisfied but it was made plain that the Lord Mayor's writ ran in the City.

The election of the Lord Mayor takes place on Michaelmas Day. The Aldermen and Masters of all Livery Companies attend a service in St Lawrence Jewry and then proceed across the yard to Guildhall. Here, Liverymen, in Common Hall assembled, are asked to express their choice for election of all Aldermen who have served the office of Sheriff. They do so once the Lord Mayor and Aldermen have withdrawn to the Livery Hall. For their first choice, the response is: 'All'; the second: 'Next Year'; and others 'Later'. This decision is conveyed to the Lord Mayor by the Recorder. With the successful candidate on his left, the Lord Mayor returns to Common Hall to the applause of the Livery. In the course of the next six weeks, there follow many official acts of recognition before Installation in the Silent Ceremony in the Guildhall on the Friday afternoon and the Declaration to the Lord Chief Justice of the Queen's Bench in the course of the Lord Mayor's Show the following day. The evening after the Investiture, a Presentation Dinner is held, usually in the Hall of the Mother Company of the Lord Mayor-elect. In the week before the Lord Mayor's Banquet, a Lighting-up Dinner is held in Guildhall to check its arrangements: the lighting, which on one occasion had failed in the event, and, especially, the menu.

The Mayoralty

Lord Mayor's Banquet: a reception and presentation beforehand in the Old Library.
The Lord Mayor 1976–7 Alderman Sir Robin Gillett Bt GBE.

The Lord Mayor and Lady Mayoress are supported by the Sheriffs and their Ladies; the Esquires; the Chaplain, the Maids of Honour and the Pikemen.

All are welcomed culminating in the finely timed entry of the Lord Chancellor, the Lord Archbishop of Canterbury and the Prime Minister.

GRACE BEFORE THE LIGHTING-UP DINNER

May this table be so well prepared and furnished
That thy Grace may light upon it now and hereafter
And all the guests be blessed.

Amen

GRACE AFTER

O Lord, of every glass and plateful
We approve — and are most grateful.

Amen

The Installation Luncheon

It is held at Mansion House before the Silent Ceremony. On this occasion, the Lord Mayor wishes his successor well in the presence of

The Mayoralty

his fellow Aldermen and their wives, and selected guests who have been involved in the legal and ceremonial rites. It is looked upon as 'the family' occasion of the year.

The menu is traditionally supposed to reflect the penury to which the Lord Mayor has been reduced by his extensive entertaining during the year: and also the hope of better things to come from the new Mayoralty. On the occasion that Sir Robin Gillett was installed. It read:

The Menu: Installation Luncheon
The Lord Mayor at his Journey's End
VALE
Sir Robin Gillett Bt GBE RD DSc RNR
AVE
Air Cdre, The Hon. Sir Peter Vanneck GBE, CB, AFC, AE, MA, DL

>The Lord Mayor at his journey's end
>Has truly little left to spend
>He longs to give a sumptious spread
>Alas, he offers up instead
>SCOTCH BROTH
>But by long custom of this City
>The next Lord Mayor tops up the kitty
>So be grateful for your second host
>When you contemplate the roast
>PARTRIDGE
>A final scrape of an empty barrel
>Brings one last dish in bright apparel
>ROBIN REDBREAST
>If you find the COFFEE lacking
>He ran out of financial backing.

Graces

It is, in fact, an occasion when the out-going and the in-coming Chaplain say Grace the one before, the other after, meat.

>GRACE BEFORE
>
>For what there is to receive, thank God.
>
>GRACE AFTER
>
>For what we have received and the promise of all the gracious hospitality of the year ensuing. Thank God.
>
>   Amen.

The Mayoralty

During this year, Sir Robin Gillett, to whom I was Chaplain, celebrated his 50th birthday. The Lady Mayoress gave a party.

GRACE

May we the Lady Libby thank
For bidding us to dine
And share with her his Lordship
At this his natal time
While thee, O Lord, we ask to bless
Our friendship, food and wine.

                                                                    Amen

Little Mansion House, Tuesday 3 December 1991
Lunch at 11 Ironmonger Lane
Lord Mayor: Sir Brian Jenkins

Eleven Ironmonger Lane was the temporary home of the Lord Mayor while Mansion House is being refurbished.

GRACE

Eleven Ironmonger Lane
Has acquired new fame
The Lord Mayor perforce must reside there
Mansion House-less betimes to abide there
With our hostess today his sparkling Lady
A blessing on their home and this table we pray Thee.

                                                                    Amen

The Mansion House

The Lord Mayor is good enough to make Mansion House, his home for the year, available for hospitality — so much so, in fact, that it is the focal point for City entertainment. Each year he holds six State Banquets: 1, the Masters and Prime Wardens of Livery Companies; 2, the Judges; 3, the Bishops; 4, the Diplomatic Corps; 5, the Arts and 6, the Bankers. There are many other civic bodies that he entertains as well as visiting business delegations from home and abroad.

Into this framework are fitted the occasions when the Liveries are given the privilege of bringing ladies and guests to their annual Company Banquet. On these occasions, the Lord Mayor and the Lady Mayoress are invited as guests in their own home. There is hardly a day in the working week when lunch and/or dinner is not served there, besides other refreshments at the numerous meetings and committees which are held in the course of the year.

The Lord Mayor is obliged to live in the Mansion House for his year in office. To that end, he is provided with a self contained flat of domestic proportions above the State Apartments. This enables him to feel at home not only there but in the whole House, despite its Justice Court-room: its prison: its extensive offices and quarters for the Esquires — the Swordbearer, the Sergeant-at-Arms and the City Marshal. He moves in on the Friday afternoon of the second Friday in November after the Silent Ceremony in Guildhall, and before his Lord Mayor's Show on the Saturday, when he is drawn in the Gold Coach through the streets to be presented to the Judges of the Queen's Bench Division at the Law Courts. He and the Lady Mayoress take tea with their predecessors who, after the Statutory Declaration, then go into purdah — leave the City for six months — until the time of the Easter Banquet.

It is a mansion of a house: grand but welcoming. One steps into an entrance hall which does not daunt the first time visitor. Only after going up the staircase are its glories progressively revealed. Though now in need of major repair, it has stood on this site since 1753. It is at the meeting point of six major thoroughfares, at the centre of the

The Mansion House

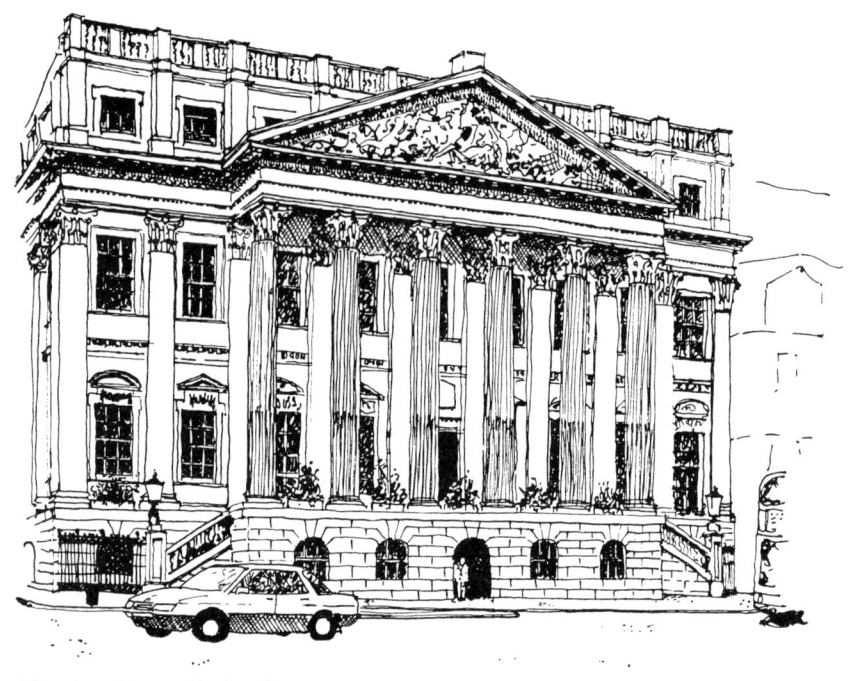

Mansion House, by kind permission of Rex S. Johnston FRIBA, President of the United Wards' Club.

City as befits its First Citizen. It was built by George Dance, a devotee of Palladio, the great Italian architect of the 16th century. He was inspired to build it with an open courtyard: inspiration, no doubt from Italy but without practical regard for the English weather.

Once that open area was roofed, however, it provided a spacious ante-room which, together with the adjacent Parlour and Drawing rooms, makes an area for receptions and pre-dinner drinks which will accommodate all those who can be seated in the Egyptian Hall.

Apart from the Guildhall, it is the only civic or Livery Hall large enough to take 400 at table. While it is undergoing its refurbishment after the celebrations scheduled for the 800th anniversary of the Mayoralty there will be a strain on the arrangements which the larger Livery Companies have been accustomed to make to entertain their members, their ladies and guests. It is on this annual occasion that Liverymen feel specially privileged to show off to friends the splendour of Mayoralty.

The Egyptian Hall, which is entered from the Salon, is beautifully proportioned, with a barrel vaulted ceiling, richly decorated and

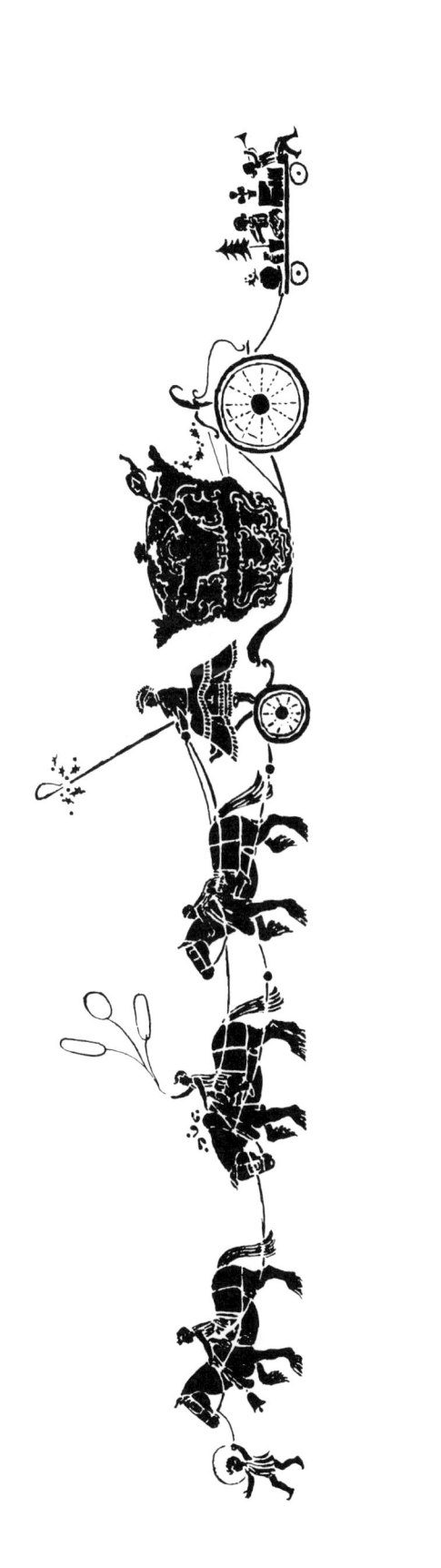

Mansion House Christmas Cards, drawn by and reproduced by kind permission of Margaret Cooke, wife of the Private Secretary to the Lord Mayor, Rear Admiral Anthony Cooke CB.
TOP The Gold Coach led by the Christ Child Procession.
BOTTOM The Esquires, the Lord Mayor and the Lady Mayoress welcome the Christ Child, with the Sheriffs and the Ladies following.

discreetly flood-lit at night. It is supported by ten columns on each side and is 80 feet high. At each end are large stained glass windows dating from 1868, the work of Alexander Gibbs. The one at the west end 'The Royal Window' depicts the signing of Magna Carta. In the lower part of it is Elizabeth I in her State Barge on the Thames. The east window 'The City Window' shows the then Lord Mayor, Sir William Walworth, quelling the Peasants Revolt of 1381 by slaying the rebel, Wat Tyler. The lower part of the window represents Edward VI entering the City after his Coronation.

The really significant feature, because of which the Hall is named Egyptian, is the surrounding gallery. Only the Egyptians, practical or philistine enough, would deface a column by using it as a gallery support! Those who gave us the Ionic, Doric or Corinthian columns never did that! We benefit, however, as the gallery forms an excellent platform for the orchestra who play there during dinner. There are certainly no better acoustics for the post horn gallop, while the whole ambience requires the Eton Boating Song in every music programme.

THE MANSION HOUSE: DINNER ROUTINE FOR LIVERY COMPANY OCCASIONS THE LOVING CUP, THE USUAL TIMING, THE TOAST LIST

When the cloakroom facilities have been used, guests ascend the staircase and receive a table seating plan before being announced by the Toastmaster.

The Master, Wardens and their Ladies receive the guests who are then served with drinks as they move on to circulate with friends and other guests in that precious half hour of the Reception. As sociability is limited after Dinner, this is the only time available to meet some of the 350 people who will be present other than those who are seated near enough at table to be within earshot. 'If you arrive on time', it is said in the City 'you are late'.

The Lord Mayor, with the civic team, joins the party fifteen minutes before the gong is sounded and dinner announced. While everyone is moving into the Egyptian Hall, the Master usually asks the Lord Mayor to pose for a photograph with those who will be processing into dinner. Gerald Sharpe is the official photographer. Painlessly and unobtrusively, he takes other pictures too which are proofed and on display in the foyer at the end of the evening.

Banquet in the Egyptian Hall, Mansion House.
Photograph by kind permission of Peter Holland.

The Mansion House

Preceded by the Beadle, the procession moves into the Hall. The orchestra strikes up and continues to play the Lord Mayor's March: SCIPIO. The ceremonial entry is made to the rhythmic hand clapping of the guests. When all have found their seats at the Top Table, the Toastmaster takes command and requests silence for the Chaplain 'who will say Grace'!

At the end of the Dinner, the Toastmaster invites all present to be upstanding and join in the singing of Grace. The words are always printed on the menu card and sung to a well known tune that gets a full-bellied response!

For these and all Thy mercies given, We bless and praise Thy name, O Lord; May we receive them with thanksgiving, Ever trusting in Thy Word: To Thee alone be honour, glory, Now and henceforth for evermore. Amen.

From the *Laudi Spirituali* AD 1545

The Mansion House

ROSE WATER BOWL

The tables are then cleared; port glasses alone remaining. Coffee cups are placed. The Rose Water Bowl is passed. These are usually large, beautifully crafted shallow bowls of silver and silver gilt. Rose petals float on the scented water into which one dips fingers or the edge of a napkin, then touching lips, temples and brows to freshen up.

The Toastmaster announces a ceremony which is integral to a City dinner:

> 'The Master and Wardens of this Worshipful Company drink to you in a Loving Cup, and bid you all a hearty welcome.'

THE LOVING CUP

So much part of the evening's togetherness is it that even when alarm was expressed at the thought of the Cup being a possible means of contracting Aids, the Livery Committee, while conceding that some might fear it as a means of transmission, decreed that the Ceremony should continue. Those having fears were invited to go through the motions without putting their lips to the Cup.

The Cups are a feature of Livery Company possessions. They are of a size that will usually take at least two pints and require the use of both hands. They always have a cap, an easily detachable lid. They are of gold, silver or silver gilt. They are filled with spiced wine: 'sack'. There is a napkin in the handle for wiping the rim after drinking.

The object of the ceremony is for each to pledge his/her loyalty to the other: in the friendship of the evening. The ceremony expresses its meaning in a ritual that reflects the one-time vulnerability of those who were drinking companions only rather than true friends. Historically, it has its focus in King Edward the Martyr's assassination on 18 March 978 at Corfe Castle while drinking from the Cup proffered by his stepmother Elfrida. She was ambitious for her own son, Ethelred ('the Unready'), to succeed to the throne and contrived that Edward should be stabbed while both his hands were engaged with the Cup leaving him unprotected from attack.

Three people now stand as the Cup is passed. When it is received, he who is then going to pledge turns to his neighbour and bows. The

The Mansion House

donor meanwhile turns to guard his back: back to back, to survey possible approaching danger. The neighbour bows, removes the lid and symbolically, as if it were a dagger ready to defend, raises it above his head. There can be no treachery in such a display of friendship. Having drunk and wiped the Cup with the attached napkin, the lid is replaced, those engaged in the action bow to each other and the Cup is passed. The process is then repeated as the previous donor sits down. With Cups on each sprig of the table, the Ceremony does not take over-long to complete. Meanwhile, the orchestra usually play such old English songs as: Drink to me only: Here's a health unto her Majesty: Love's Old Sweet Song.

Port decanters are placed before the Master and at the end of the sprigs. Their stoppers are removed simultaneously taking the timing from the Master. The port is passed, gentlemen frequently helping the lady on his left before passing the decanter. The port circulates. Brandies and liqueurs are offered — and cigars. Coffee is offered after the Loyal Toast. The staff then withdraw. The Toasts are pledged and speeches made.

THE TOAST LIST
(as usually followed on Civic and Livery occasions)

When the tables have been cleared and the port passed, the Toastmaster gavels. The Master stands. All stand. There is no allocution. The Master proposes:

The Queen

The band plays the first verse of the National Anthem (singing optional). Glasses are raised from the table and the pledge is made:

The Queen

Smoking is then permitted; 'those who must, may'. The next toast follows almost immediately. It is conventional, as a mark of unique respect for the Monarch, to sit briefly after the Loyal Toast and before the Toast to the Royal Family. The Master's proposition:

> Queen Elizabeth, The Queen Mother
> The Prince Philip, Duke of Edinburgh
> The Prince and Princess of Wales
>   and the other members of the Royal Family

The Mansion House

The presence of the definite article in the Toast is to be noted: this is not 'other' but 'the other' members.

The first half of a verse of the National Anthem is played. No singing. Glasses are raised from the table:

> The Royal Family

A longer pause follows during which coffee is served, before the Master, a Warden or other chosen Member of Livery proposes:

> The Lord Mayor
> The Corporation of London
>   and the Sheriffs

The Toast is repeated when the response is made. If the Lord Mayor is present, he replies.

After a relaxed pause, the Toastmaster enquires of the Master whether he should continue with the remaining Toasts, adding sotto voce 'or shall we let them enjoy themselves for a little longer'.

> The Worshipful Company of XYZ
> 'Root and branch may it continue and flourish
> for ever, coupled with the name of the Master'

Usually proposed by a friend of the Master. Response by the Master who will propose the Toast to:

> The Guests

The response is usually made by a well-known personality and after-dinner speaker. His allocution:

> 'Master, My Lord Mayor, My Lords, Alderman,
> Mr Recorder, Sheriffs, Liverymen, Ladies and Gentlemen'

Speeches are usually, and hopefully geared to the notice on the invitation card: Carriages: 1030.

> The Toastmaster: 'Ladies and Gentlemen. That concludes the official proceedings for the evening. The Master has asked me to say that there is a stirrup cup available in the ante room for any who care to join him'.

The Mansion House

THE USUAL TIMING OF THE DINNER ROUTINE

Invitations are mostly timed at 7pm for 7.30. It is often remarked that if you arrive on time in the City you are late.

7.00 pm	The Master and Wardens receive the Guests
7.15 pm	The arrival of the Lord Mayor and the Civic Party
7.25 pm	Toastmaster announces dinner
7.35 pm	Dinner commences: the Toastmaster gavelling and announcing Grace.
9.00 pm	Grace is sung. *Laudi Spirituali*
	The Toastmaster announces the Loving Cup: 'The Master and Wardens of this Worshipful Company drink to you in a Loving Cup and bid you all a hearty welcome'.
9.15 pm	The Loyal Toasts
9.20 pm	The Civic Toast
9.30 pm	Reply by the Lord Mayor who will propose the Toast to the Company
9.45 pm	Reply by the Master who will propose the Toast to the Guests
10.00 pm	Reply by the invited guest speaker
10.15 pm	The Toastmaster asks the guests to be upstanding while the Master and his distinguished Guests withdraw. He announces the availability of a Stirrup Cup.

Graces on Some Committee Occasions

CITY LANDS AND BRIDGE HOUSE ESTATES COMMITTEE

The Senior Committee whose Chairman is Chief Commoner. His annual dinner is in honour of the previous Chairman.

Chief Commoner: Mr Deputy B L Morgan CBE

GRACE 1978

Lord who did bless the loaves and fishes
And doubtless Ring and Brymer's dishes
Grant now to all our Bunny's guests
Good food and fellowship as he behests
To Chiefs who've passed the Chair like Steiner
And lesser mortals, each honoured diner
May we, O Lord, raise thankful hands
To Thee — and all of City Lands.

Amen

Note
This Dinner was held in honour of Frank Steiner. He is a solicitor, clerk to several Livery Companies, high ranking Mason and was courageously supported by Joyce, his severely handicapped wife. He made a great contribution to City life and was fittingly thanked by its best known citizen, Bunny Morgan, Honorary Secretary of the City Livery Club.

GRACE 1979

Chief Commoners come and Chief Commoners go
But everyone is delighted to see them
Especially tonight, when they're dined with delight
By successors to whom they've been Chairmen.
So Lord it's a blessing we ask as we sit down to dine
Not so much on the table with its good food and wine

Graces on Some Committee Occasions

But on men whose high praises should be sung to an organ
Like our ubiquitous, ebullient, good friend — Bunny Morgan.

Amen

GRACE 1980

'A loaf of bread' the Walrus said
'Is what we chiefly need
'Pepper and vinegar besides are very good indeed'.
But as Pat Roney offers more
His menu's good to read
We'll let the oysters go, O Lord
And being blessed, we'll feed.

Amen

Note
This dinner was held in Carpenters' Hall.

GRACE 1981

At Fishmongers' Hall we're gathered in total accord
His service to the City of Tom to applaud
For all he has done
And the Honour he's won
We give thanks, asking a blessing, O Lord.

Amen

Note
Principal guests were past Chief Commoners. Among the most illustrious was Sir Kingsley Collett, who bestrode the City like a colossus, and is affectionately known as Tom. His award of a Doctorate at City University was celebrated at Fishmongers' Hall.

GRACE 1982

Tonight City Lands stand before you O Lord
As they dine at the premier Livery's board
The Chief's done the test
There's nothing but best
Giving a menu we'll be sure to applaud.

Amen

Graces on Some Committee Occasions

Note

The premier and most prestigious company is the Mercers. One of its best known Liverymen was Dick Whittington.

> GRACE 1983
>
> O Lord, graciously bless our repast
> And o'er the CV of your host kindly cast
> An eye that will see
> What was once GLC
> Is now as City as Chiefs of the past.
>
> Amen

Note

The host was Joseph Brown who was a most able Chief Commoner. He had previously been Vice Chairman of the GLC 1970–71, also Sheriff 1977–78.

> GRACE 1984
>
> The man condemned did eat in haste whatever he could carry
> But we, O Lord, are different, here to linger and to tarry
> In the purlieus of Old Bailey
> It'll be the best with gravy
> Provided by our reigning Chief, the magisterial Harry.
>
> Amen

Note

The Dinner was exceptionally held in the Grand Hall of the Old Bailey and hosted by Harry Duckworth, a dedicated magistrate.

Dinner held in Clothworkers' Hall,
Wednesday 12 October 1988
Hosted by Chairman: A Brian Wilson Esq
In Honour of Edwina Coven CBE JP DL Deputy

> GRACE
>
> Traditions have been made and customs broken
> By that Lady the exceptional Edwina Coven
> She was the first to be Chief
> From the Police having taken her leaf
> Bless us, Lord, and the dreams she has woven.
>
> Amen

Graces on Some Committee Occasions

Note

Mrs Edwina Coven was the first lady Chief Commoner having graduated through a long held chairmanship of the Police Committee. This dinner sadly remains notable for being the first public function to fall victim to the recent outbreak of Salmonella poisoning. Over 100 were infected including Mrs Coven's husband, Frank, who spent five days in the London Clinic.

COAL, CORN AND RATES
FINANCE COMMITTEE
The Examination of Securities Dinner

This Dinner is held annually after the Bank of England has examined the Corporation's Securities

GRACE 1975

For uncooked books and peace of mind
For Fellowship, being fed and wined
For talk and speech
Griggs — Keith — each
We thank Thee, Lord, for being dined.

Amen

Note
John Griggs: Chamberlain
James Keith: Chairman C C R Committee — the City's Chancellor of the Exchequer.

GRACE 1978

They've examined our Securities
They've gone at them like leeches
And found them in good order, Lord
Deserving of fair speeches
Economies that did the trick
Will make this meal the richer
So good friends all
In Saddlers' Hall
Thank God for Griggs and Stitcher.

Amen

Graces on Some Committee Occasions

GRACE 1979

We've the Lord Mayor and Sheriffs to toast
By a Chairman who's the most generous host
But before we all sit I'm going to pray
In what, Lord is intended as a suppliant's way
That the finance of our Coal, our Corn and our Rates
May still leave what is best to go on our plates.

                                                            Amen

GRACE 1980

As always, Lord, we offer Thee
Our praise for all we eat for free
Especially when we're in the clear
With Auditors another year
Allow us then to offer thanks
To Coal and Corn and Rates Finance.

                                                            Amen

GRACE 1981

It's for the third and last time of asking, Lord
That Gerald, our Chairman, seeks your accord
In the form of a blessing on ledger and board
Coal, Corn and Rates commend what he's done
The golden opinions he's courageously won
But tonight we all pray
As the 'guidelines' give way
He'll relax and enjoy the good things to come.

                                                            Amen

Note

Gerald Stitcher was Chairman during the financial troubles of the Seventies, and when the first Thatcher administration requested the observance of 'guidelines'. 'The good things to come' — he went on to become Chief Commoner, though not before he had open heart surgery.

GRACE 1981

Thou knowest, Lord, that we rate this the best:
The Dinner that is especially blessed
While one of our hosts is now an old crony
The other's a new boy, by name Patrick Roney

Graces on Some Committee Occasions

Together they've concocted as we read on the menu
All delights of the table in this special venue
It is though our prayer as we sit down to dine
When the books of our lives have been checked line by line
That like them we'll be given for passing our test
Nothing less than what goes with good wine at its best.

              Amen

Note

Mr Deputy Patrick Roney succeeded Gerald Stitcher as Chairman.

GRACE 1982

Lord grace the good helpings to be served on our plates
And in Saddler's stemmed glasses, wines, all of them, greats
For when the year's work is done
Pat Roney likes fun
With his guests and committee of Coal, Corn and Rates.

              Amen

GRACE 1983

We've all had our champers, our sherry, our gin
And now, Lord, on the solids we're about to begin
Along with the Chief Cashier of the Bank
We're humbly aware that we have You to thank
That Securities examined have not, nay could not, prove phony
While they're kept by the skill of John Griggs and Pat Roney.

              Amen

GRACE 1984

It's the Chamberlain and Chairman, Lord,
Who've enabled us once more to afford
This best meal in town
To which we're about to sit down
When I've said with approval from our John and Pat
Benedictus Dominum Benedicat.

              Amen

Graces on Some Committee Occasions

GRACE 1985

John Griggs and Pat Roney will again do us well
And in asking God's blessing I'm happy to tell
Its been better each year
That's why we're all here
Though tonight, and most sadly, it's our John's farewell.

            Amen

GRACE 1986

What fun it is, Lord, with Pat Roney to dine
For he never objects to the Vicar's odd rhyme
But believes that a laugh
With a stiff 'other half'
Adds grace to what's always a jolly good time.

            Amen

Note

This was a Grace somewhat directed at 'the misery brigade' who disliked the bad doggerel and my even worse approach to these occasions. My Graces were intended to make a grateful offering of a merry heart. They sometimes evoked a standing ovation from those who were, of course, on their feet.

GRACE

On the Chancellor struggling with inflationary deals
And the Bank learning, without 'corsets' just how it feels
The City, O Lord, that's Coal, Corn and Rates
Pat Roney's mates
Asks a blessing in a Grace before meals.

            Amen

Note

Corsets and inflation were topical.

GRACE

Coal, Corn and Rates — Finance men, not the trendy and arty
Though their Chairman now has in tandem Bernard P Harty
Together they've examined the books
Wisely engaged John Coomb and his Cooks
So, if it pleases you, Lord, we should still have a good Party.

            Amen

Graces on Some Committee Occasions

Note
Bernard P Harty succeeded John Griggs as Chamberlain in 1983.

GRACE

'Twas fish the mongers checked out here
On their doorstep at Billingsgate year after year
But tonight it's not fish
At the Chamberlain's wish
But the Cash, the Securities, the Lolly, O Lord
That examined, a blessing may add to our board.

                                                         Amen

Note
The Dinner was held at Fishmongers' Hall near the Old Billingsgate Market in the year that the Fish Market was transferred to the Isle of Dogs.

BILLINGSGATE AND LEADENHALL MARKET COMMITTEE

The Fish Market, traditionally trading from Billingsgate, moved to the Isle of Dogs in 1982. Some 2500 people are employed and handle up to 750 tonnes of fish each week.

GRACE 1982

O Lord who blessed the loaves and fishes
Be pleased to grant our Chairman's wishes
That Billingsgate though 'dogged' may be
More fishes from our coastal sea
May sell
For truth to tell
With chips it's still the best of Britain's native dishes.

                                                         Amen

GRACE 1983

The Isle of Dogs has become the in-place for fishes
And as such has fulfilled all Billingsgate wishes
So, good Lord, we give praise
To our Ivy, and raise
A prayer that will bless us and all of her dishes.

                                                         Amen

Graces on Some Committee Occasions

Note

Mrs Ivy Sharpe was a popular Lady Chairman who made sure that the traders were pleased with their new surroundings.

WEST HAM PARK COMMITTEE

Eight members of the Corporation, three from the local Parish Church and four from the Gurney family to whom Ham House belonged in the mid-nineteenth century, form the Committee of Management of the Estate, some 77 acres in extent. The estate, now called West Ham Park, is held by the Corporation in trust for ever 'as open public grounds and gardens for the resort and recreation of adults and as play grounds for children and youth'.

Adjoining the park is the Corporation's nursery, where plants are grown for use in other parks and for special functions at Guildhall and Mansion House. Like Epping Forest, Burnham Beeches, Highgate Wood and Kent and Surrey Commons, this is part of the pioneering foresight used by the City to acquire, out of non-public funds, and maintain open spaces for the benefit of the citizens of our urban areas.

> GRACE
> Our host, Wimburn Horlock, has now made his mark
> In the way that he's chaired the great West Ham Park
> So, Lord, in this crypt let your blessing be given
> On the lunch he provides for all who have striven
> To enhance with the gardener's most excellent blooms
> The sight of our tables sparkling with knives, forks and spoons.
>
> Amen

THE HOUSING COMMITTEE

The Corporation owns and administers flats and houses not just in the City but in the Boroughs on both sides of the river. Much of the property originally belonged to the Bridge House Estates. It has all been modernised and equipped to cater for all ages, including the retired and severely handicapped. The Corporation is a model landlord in this sphere.

Graces on Some Committee Occasions

GRACE

We ask a blessing O Lord
For others' bed and their daily board
The work of the Housing Committee
Let us sit down to dine
On his good food and wine
Being grateful to Chairman Donnelly.

                                                                Amen

THE GENERAL PURPOSES COMMITTEE

Mansion House, 7 July 1978
Chairman: H J Spurrier

GRACE

It's Mansion House they care for
That's why we're here O Lord
Its Standing Orders, Lord Mayor's Coach
And City Vicars too
That G P, jack of all trades, has annually to do
So bless them in their labours and these Thy gifts as well
That Thine shall be the glory their many works forth tell.

                                                                Amen

THE POLICE COMMITTEE

Ivan Luckin was in the chair at the time of the major police review when numbers and morale improved enormously. He was also responsible for persuading the Americans to buy Rennie's London Bridge and move it stone by stone to Lake Havasu in the Arizona desert. It has been a great commercial success, not least because of the pub built at the end of the Bridge and selling English ale. The purchasers, so it is said, thought that they were buying the distinctive structure of Tower Bridge. The grime, which they also thought gave the Bridge historic London authenticity, has been made sparkling clean by the blown sand of the desert.

GRACE

His lot is not a happy one, so it is said O Lord
We ask a special blessing then on Ivan Luckin's board

Graces on Some Committee Occasions

That the work of his committee
For the Police of this great City
Will cover our protection and keep us free from fraud.
Amen

GRACE

Ivan Luckin, past Chairman, golden opinions has won
For confounding Gilbert's notion of the unhappy one
He also sold our Bridge to the Yanks
For a million or more, and our thanks
For seeing as well that our coppers
No longer are down on their uppers
We've very good reasons to thank him today
As on our tables and guests a blessing we pray.
Amen

THE LIBRARY COMMITTEE

Chairman: David Shalit

GRACE

Our Chairman knows how much it costs
To feed the mind with books
Thank God, say we
From what we see
He's not counted the cost of cooks.
Amen

Chairman: John Holland

GRACE

We feed the mind these days, O Lord
From libraries of books
Our diet's what we can afford
And Ring and Brymer's cooks.
Amen

Graces on Some Committee Occasions

THE ESTABLISHMENT COMMITTEE

GRACE

O Lord with your blessing we'll be divinely content
With a dinner that needs no compliment
Though it may make us fatter
'It's people that matter'
So says the Lord Mayor when benevolent.

                                                          Amen

Note

The Lord Mayor's slogan for the year.

GRACE

It's the Establishment Committee who in fellowship meet
Asking your blessing, Lord, on what we shall eat
And for the jobs that we've got
Which is our lucky lot
We give thanks as we now take our seat.

                                                          Amen

Note

Chairman: Henry Duckworth. Dinner was held in the Old Library, Guildhall. It was in 1981, a time when the unemployment figures were rising, to almost 3 million.

THE SPITALFIELDS MARKET COMMITTEE
Lunch at Guildhall in the Old Library, Wednesday 2 November 1988
Chairman: A John James Esq

GRACE

Spitalfields
Fruit and vegetables yields
To feed the Lord Mayor at this lunch
For John James in the chair
We offer a prayer
So we'll all enjoy what he gives us to munch.

                                                          Amen

Graces on Sundry Occasions

ROYAL GRACES

HM The Queen Mother
The Shipwrights' Company, 27 February 1990
Court Lunch at Ironmongers' Hall
The Prime Warden: Michael Everard

In honour of the 90th birthday of HM The Queen Mother and attended by HRH The Prince Philip, the Duke of Edinburgh: Permanent Master of the Shipwrights' Company.

>GRACE
>
>God be praised
>As our hearts are raised
>By our youngest Liveryman the Royal Lady
>May our victuals be blessed
>Our wine at its best
>Our permanent Master, well pleased, Lord, we pray thee.
>
>>Amen

Farmers' and Fletchers' Hall, 9 June 1987
HRH The Princess Royal
Master: A N Taylor

A luncheon following the official opening of Farmers' and Fletchers' Hall by The Princess Royal.

>GRACE
>
>When Farmers and Fletchers fraternise
>To build a Hall of this elegant size
>And a Princess sheds such a royal ray
>Over the opening proceedings of this special day
>We pray a Grace on our food and our wine
>And a blessing on each time we sit down to dine.
>
>>Amen

Graces on Sundry Occasions

Ladies Banquet: Wednesday 18 May 1983 at Launderers' Hall
Guest of Honour: HRH The Princess Royal
Master: Richard Seaman

GRACE

It's our home, Lord, where we're dining tonight
To honour our guests, and hopefully delight
HRH with our craft and our dressing
Our shirts starched and ironed and whiter than white
Our napkins, fair linen, all pressed till they're right
All we ask, good Lord, now — is your blessing.

Livery Lunch, The Loriners' Company
December 1979 at Barber Surgeons' Hall
Master: John Hovey

GRACE

We're asking a blessing, O Lord, on a menu
That's in tasty accord with this modern venue
And also we pray
In a Loriner's way
That our bits and bridles and spurs
May be usefully hers
Whom we've clothed in our Livery today.

              Amen

Note

Lunch followed the Court Meeting at which HRH the Princess Anne the Princess Royal — was clothed in the Livery. When introduced to her before lunch, I expressed the hope that she would not mind a passing reference in the Grace. 'As long as it doesn't spoil the food', she said with a permissive chuckle.

Goldsmiths' Hall — Builders' (later Constructors') Company
Guest of Honour: HRH The Duke of Gloucester
Master: Brian Scruby

GRACE

By courtesy of Goldsmiths, O Lord, it's the Builders this time
Who here with Royalty are privileged to dine
And we're asking your blessing in this gracious venue

Graces on Sundry Occasions

On the gastronomic delights of this promising menu
And we pray that the Master and all of his guests
Will find that this evening is most happily blest.
                                                    Amen

During dinner, the Master, Brian Scruby, sent me a note to say that HRH enjoyed the Grace and that, if I would see him afterwards, he would trade one for one. 'One good Grace deserves another' said HRH. 'It may sound a bit scurrilous, but it is a good Scots Presbyterian Grace. You may be able to use it.' I have . . . often (vide Old Bailey).

Good food, Good meet, Good God — Let's eat.

Ironmongers' Hall — Tuesday 9th February 1993
Shipwrights Livery Dinner
Permanent Master: HRH The Duke of Edinburgh
The Prime Warden: David I Moor
Guest of Honour: HRH The Duke of York

GRACE

There's a Royal tradition and proud pedigree
That a son of the line is a man of the sea
We rejoice then tonight as for us that holds good
And ask Lord to bless him in our wine and our food
Keep him too ever mindful that his master — is rather
One fraternally and happily dubbed 'permanent father'.
                                                    Amen

On the occasion when HRH Prince Charles had been elected to the Court of the Shipwrights he had responded to Prince Philip's speech of congratulations by addressing him as 'permanent — father'.

ANNIVERSARIES

Derek and Joan Kemp
Silver Wedding Anniversary
Armoury House, 31 March 1981

Derek and Joan have been family friends since our earliest days in the City. He is one of its great entrepreneurs. They have brought their family up within its corporate life. They are devoted to its traditions.

Graces on Sundry Occasions

GRACE

O Lord who brought joy to a bride and groom
As you mingled with friends and all in the room
So now as we're gathered with special intent
To help Derek and Joan recall that event
We ask for your blessing on what they're beholden
And pray that what's Silver will one day be Golden.

Amen

Melanie and Nigel Andrew
Wedding Breakfast
Los Dos Leones, Barcelona, Saturday 1 October 1988

GRACE

It was at Cana of Galilee that the water was blest
And the resulting wine was vintage, the best
And here now Lord, on this wedding day
It's your blessing we pray
Not just on the goodies we're about to enjoy
But on the ravishing Melanie and her lucky boy.

Amen

Behind the Grace is the somewhat unlikely story of the Anglican Vicar being involved in Catholic Spain (in the church of Santa Maria De La Bonanova, Barcelona) with a Roman Priest in the marriage service of an Irish Colleen to a traditional son of the C of E. Melanie is the daughter of Frances and Alan Plant who have lived in Barcelona for the past five years. He works from there throughout Europe as the representative of Massey Fergusson.

Twelve years ago, I was on a ski-ing holiday alone: my wife, suffering from hyperthermia, had felt unable to go but did not prevent me from doing so.

On the first evening, after a day on the slopes, I was approached by Alan as I stood at the bar. In friendly conversation, he tried to find out who I was and what I did. It was an intimate and small 15 bed hotel at Chateau D'Oeux. I suddenly feared that if I said that I was a parson nobody there might even treat me as human for the rest of the fortnight. 'Something in the City' I told him. On the second evening, he and Frances, his vivacious and beautiful wife, again were pleasantly inquisitive. 'A retired Naval Officer living in the City', I volunteered this time and proceeded to talk enthusiastically about Barbican.

Graces on Sundry Occasions

The late Pat Reid, author of the Colditz story, was the other singleton in the hotel. We shared a table, but he was out for dinner that night. I sat alone. Halfway through dinner, Melanie aged 14, presented herself. A blue eyed blonde with her hair done up in a top knot with a red ribbon, she looked just like the incarnation of the fairy at the top of our Christmas tree. 'With mummy and daddy's compliments. They are sad to see you sitting alone and wondered whether you would like to join them for coffee and a brandy at the end of the meal.'

'I will be delighted, especially if you are going to be there.' As I joined them, I made apologetic noises in terms of being somewhat economical with the truth. I had not told an untruth on either occasion but I had told less than the truth.

'What I am in the City is a parson' said I when seated and feeling at ease with them. 'I sensed there was something different and not unfamiliar' said Alan; 'my father was a parson too'. For the next seven winters, they have kindly invited me to join up with them and to deepen a great family friendship.

So it came to pass, in the fullness of time, I married the most ravishing fairy from the top of any Christmas tree. In 1991 I christened their first born, and in 1992 there will be a second.

Dinner to celebrate the 80th Birthday of
 the Rt Hon J Enoch Powell
The Ballroom, Hyde Park Hotel, Monday 22 June 1992
Host: The Marquis of Salisbury

> GRACE
>
> It's not in Latin, Hebrew, Greek or other tongues that scholars speak
> That Grace is offered here tonight. But it's a special blessing that we seek
> In English, beloved of him whose four score years extol his native land
> Whom we now honour, Lord, with thanks for all the bounties of your hand.
>
> Amen

Note
He and Pam liked and thanked me for the unexpected Grace: 'Didn't know you were a poet'.

Graces on Sundry Occasions

It was an honour to be among his selected friends. It was also memorable for me because it was the one night in perhaps two hundred occasions on the road home before midnight that I was breathalysed. Fortunately the wine waiter had not been in such pressing attendance as at a livery dinner. The police could not get the needle out of the amber on their machine. Amused, they asked me, in parson's evening dress collar, what I had going for me!

Lunch to celebrate the 65th birthday of Mrs Hobart Moore
South House, Cranleigh, Sunday 13th September 1992

Brenda gave a large party in a marquee in her garden to celebrate her 'coming of age'.

> GRACE
>
> Family and friends from far and wide
> Wish that Brenda had Hoby today at her side
> We all love and admire her for what she has done
> And the new lease on life which she's just begun
> Lord, bless all these goodies which she offers today
> And keep her in health, wealth and beauty — what we
>   now pray.
>
> Amen

A number of our friends, whose marriages were probably somewhat hastened by the outbreak of War, held their anniversaries in 1989–1990.

Charles and Cathy Coward
Golden Wedding Anniversary, 9 July 1988
Lunch given at the Farmers' and Fletchers' Hall

> GRACE
>
> Today, Lord, we gather with special intent
> To help two good friends gratefully observe their life's
>   journey's event
> They've been cheered by their Clive over most of its miles
> With Frances, JJ, Tamsin and Giles
> But our Charles could not have achieved it, not even he
> Without the enduring love of his devoted Cathy.
>
> Amen

Graces on Sundry Occasions

Joe and Vera Brown
Golden Wedding Anniversary, 9 September 1989
Lunch at the Farmers' and Fletchers' Hall

GRACE

Deo Gratias
Believe it or not they've had the lot
Silver, Ruby and Golden
And we, honoured guests are here (presents verboten)
To give thanks for all life has given
The lovely things for which they've both striven
How glad we are to be with our dear Vera and Joe
To enjoy their hospitality now graced, with wine ready to flow.

Amen

Vera usually sends me a little ditty in the course of a meal. She is a ready and expert versifier.

Sweet Basil's a herb of much grace
It adds spicy savour to meat
Our Basil gives grace when we eat
But verbal — not herbal.

Harry and Mary Duckworth
Golden Wedding Anniversary, 24 June 1990
Lunch at The Lodge, Southgate

GRACE

Mary Mary was not contrary when Harry gave her a whirl
He's since turned that wartime bride into his golden girl
He's achieved everything else too in the greatest style
Magistrate — CBE — CC and PM of our City's Square Mile
To our congratulations then add your blessing good Lord
On all of us the delights of their anniversary board.

Amen

Graces on Sundry Occasions

Stanley and Aida Flintham
Golden Wedding Anniversary, 16 September 1989
Lunch at Farmers' and Fletchers' Hall

> GRACE
>
> Happy are we to be keeping their golden day
> With 'the Flinthams' in this typically generous way
> Stanley has already given so much to the City
> That there's no need to dwell on that part in my ditty
> As he wants us to thank the good Lord for their many blessings in life
> Especially of course for Aida that incomparable helpmate, his wife.
>
> Amen

Sir Lindsay and Hazel Ring
Golden Wedding Anniversary, 8 June 1990
Lunch at Armourers' and Brasiers'

> GRACE
>
> Amorous (Armourers) and Brassieres (Brasiers) is what they affectionately say
> And where more appropriate to keep this Golden Day
> As with Lindsay and Hazel we gather to cheer
> Times past, and that so special year
> When they gave us such fun. So bless them good Lord
> And the very special dishes of their anniversary board.
>
> Amen

Sir Lindsay Ring was Lord Mayor 1975–6. Ring (and Brymer's) dishes have been a special feature of City catering over many years. He is a Liveryman of the Armourers' and Brasiers' Company.

CELEBRATIONS

A Celebration Dinner given by Arthur Kennedy OBE
Tallow Chandlers' Hall, 4 December 1991

> GRACE
>
> Friends join with Arthur in his Order of Chivalry
> To celebrate, what we all rejoice in, his special OBE
> It's been uniquely won

Graces on Sundry Occasions

>For all the varied laundering done
>So a bumper blessing, Lord, on him we now pray Thee.
>>Amen

Arthur Kennedy is a Founder Member of the Worshipful Company of Launderers. He was Master in 1977–8 when the Grant of Livery was made. From modest beginnings in the industry he worked his way into being one of its great captains: serving it, in all aspects of its activity, over the years. He is a most popular character and everyone delighted in his award.

Guildhall Lodge No 3116
Installation Dinner, Wednesday 27 May 1992

>GRACE
>
>We're in company with Gog & Magog, with Winston, Nelson and Pitt
>As among our nation's heroes we're now privileged to sit
>To enjoy the food and friendship of this our Festive Board
>And mindful of all others be grateful to our Lord.
>>Amen

The Installation was of the Rt Hon The Lord Mayor, Sir Brian Jenkins GBE MA DSc, a Past Grand Swordbearer, by the Grand Master, Most Worshipful Brother, His Royal Highness, the Duke of Kent KG GCMG GCVO ADC. There were 374 Brethren at the ceremony in the Old Library, with a reception in the Crypt, followed by the Dinner in Guildhall.

AMERICAN THANKSGIVING DAY

Tom Nangle, alas now the late Tom Nangle, partner in Shearman & Stirling of 53 Wall Street, New York, practised for his firm in EC2 for some years. He had a great capacity for friendship among his contemporaries in City law firms, and committed himself to the corporate life of the Square Mile wholeheartedly, becoming President of the Bassishaw Ward Club, doubtless the only American ever to achieve such distinction. His nostalgia for the years spent here has brought him back from New York, somewhat paradoxically, each Thanksgiving Day. All his friends here are bidden to lunch in a private room either at the Savoy or the Travellers Club. Needless to say, it is one of those dates that all of us provisionally carry forward in our diaries from year to year.

Graces on Sundry Occasions

Part of the after lunch ritual is the reading of Art Buchwald's classic: 'Explaining Thanksgiving to the French'. It is reprinted each year in the International New York Herald Tribune. It was written to be read aloud. Lawyers have more than enough 'French' to savour its wit. It is a great party. In his honour his friends have carried it on each year since his death.

GRACE

It was our kinsmen, O Lord, who once left us
But who nearly went short
Of Turkey and Port
Until they gave thanks and were gracious
And as for this day
It's a blessing we pray
On Tom Nangle & Co
Who still love us so
That they come back each year to befriend us.

                  Amen

I have a reciprocal love for America. Invited to make one of a team of twenty preachers of all denominations, I first went to the States in 1968 and returned each August for the next 17 years. My appointments on that first trip were to Boston; New York; then two weeks in Boise, Idaho; before returning to Washington for my last Sunday. I could not find Boise, Idaho on the map. I enquired about it from a young US naval cadet at Dartmouth (where I was then Chaplain) on exchange from Annapolis. 'You can't go there; it's a potato patch.'

When I queried the appropriateness of the appointment with the English Speaking Union, who were promoting the tour team, they informed me that I was being honoured in going there; 'it is the Cathedral of the Rockies; filled twice over (2,500 each time) every Sunday morning; the Vicar has been voted Clergyman of the Year'. I would, in their opinion, be missing an opportunity. . . . I went back there for the next seven years. When the Vicar was promoted to the University capital of Oregon, Eugene, he invited me to follow him there for the next six years in August. After he retired, I returned to marry, to baptise and to become a godparent. I am a West Coast man. I delight in being recently elected to The Pilgrims.

Washington became a stop over. On one occasion, I preached in The National Presbyterian Church, known as Eisenhower's Church, in

Graces on Sundry Occasions

Nebraska Avenue. In the glad-handing process, as the congregation filed out of Church, I was asked for a copy of my sermon for printing in the *Record*. (That was a title in the religious Press here which, as far as I knew, had a miniscule circulation.) I appreciated the implied approval but regretted that, as my host had laid on a lunch for forty people and an afternoon programme, I would be unable to write it up from the notes from which I had preached.

After he had passed, the Minister, standing a little distance away, came across and asked what Senator Stennis had been saying. 'There are not many American clergy who get reported in the *Congressional Record*, he said, 'I would ask your host to cancel his arrangements for you this afternoon and get yourself writing'. Senator Stennis was Chairman of the Armed Services Committee, and was as good as his word.

SERMON TO REMEMBER

Mr Stennis. Mr President, recently it was my privilege to hear an outstanding and challenging sermon delivered at the National Presbyterian Church in Washington by Revd. Basil Watson, a visiting Minister from London, England. Revd. Watson is a member of the British Navy and is the Chaplain of the British Naval College in London. The sermon reflects the fine character and spiritual strength of Revd. Watson and shows also a broad understanding of the practical problems that face us not only in England but also in America and elsewhere. I ask unanimous consent to have the sermon printed in the Record.

There being no objection, the sermon was ordered to be printed in the Record.

LUNCH AT THE OLD BAILEY

Some people have the great good fortune to be invited to lunch at the Old Bailey and to get an insider's view of a Judge's day. Guests sit down to table with them as well as seeing them at work in the courtroom. The Lord Mayor, who is the principal Magistrate of the City, is also responsible for the efficient working of the Central Criminal Court, as the Old Bailey has been officially called since 1834. The Lord Mayor is represented there each day by an Alderman, while the Sheriff on duty

Graces on Sundry Occasions

acts as host to his guests, as indeed he does to all the Judges. One is usually invited to the Sheriff's suite of rooms in good time to join the Judges in the library at 13.00. They will have been in court all morning and return at 14.00. They remain gowned and wigged over the lunch hour. In scarlet are the High Court Judges, as is the Recorder of London, with a distinctive blue orphrey to his gown. In black are the County Court Judges and the Recorders. Guests are seated among them and either get caught up in cross table general conversation on some legal query, or in personal talk leading to a most agreeable invitation to go into Court for some part of the afternoon session.

Knowing that time is of the essence of the lunch break, I have found from experience that brevity in Grace produces the most spirited Amen. When I used the Scottish Presbyterian Grace taught me by HRH The Duke of Gloucester (*vide:* Constructors) I also saw immediate note being made, doubtless for future use at the Golf Club!

Good food, Good meet, Good God, Let's eat

The Recorder, Sir James Miskin, often raises a laugh at my expense when I've 'spoken' before some dinner and he afterwards. He tells of the occasion at the Bailey when I'm reputed to have been guilty of a spoonerism: 'Bless these gifts to our use and keep us ever needful of the minds of others'. Whenever I pass the formidable walls of the Old Bailey, I think with pleasure of the warm humanity of the men whose job it is to dispense justice. Such thoughts inevitably flip the mind back to Judge Jeffries and others who dealt with the criminals of the notorious Newgate Prison in the Sessions House which, until 1774, stood alongside it on the present site. It cannot be said that today, since the abolition of the death penalty, mistakenly I think, that they do not dispense justice with mercy. It is significant that it is the gracious Lady of Justice who caps the dome of the Bailey and has done so since 1907. She was sculpted by Frederick Williams Pomeroy and is perhaps one of the world's most famed works of the art.

My host on Monday 30 November 1987 was the Sheriff, Mr Richard Saunders. What gave added pleasure to the occasion was a friendship over the years. He was my Churchwarden. His office was next door to the Church. I see him frequently through the Chartered Surveyors (*vide:* the Company). Both he and his wife are dedicated to various forms of service to the City. It was very satisfying to see him as Sheriff so much at home with the Judges. The seating plan for the occasion is on the facing page.

Graces on Sundry Occasions

The Reverend Basil Watson, Dr John Caldwell, Mrs Amanda Jackson
Monday 30 November 1987
Central Criminal Court, Luncheon

Alderman Sir Christopher Leaver

Mr Justice Farquarson	Judge Coombe
Judge Denison	Judge Lymbery
Judge Quarren Evans	Judge Petre
The Revd. Basil Watson	Judge Smedley
Mr Recorder Gray	Mr Justice Alliott
Mr Justice McNeill	Mr Sheriff Richard Saunders
Dr John Cardwell	Mr Recorder Spencer
Mr Recorder Rawley	Judge Richard Lowry
Judge Argyle	Judge Capstick
Mrs Amanda Jackson	Judge Machin
Judge Rant	Courts Administrator G F Addicott Esq
Group Captain John Constable	

Secondary and Under Sheriff
Colonel L. B. A. Thacker

GRACE WILL BE SAID

BOVIS 1885–1985
CENTENARY LUNCH

A Lunch was held at Mansion House to mark the centenary of this International Construction and Civil Engineering firm, which is also

Graces on Sundry Occasions

involved in the building and property market. Its emblem is a woodpecker.

I was invited to say Grace by a director, a good friend, John Gillam, whom I had got to know through the Amicables — that dining club, famed for its urbanity and wit, and limited to 40 Old Boys of Christ's Hospital School. Such an invitation is a rare honour.

GRACE

Bovis ask a blessing, O Lord, as we sit down to dine
On Mansion House food and the fruit of the vine
That they may build and construct at home and abroad
And pecker their way through the toughest of board
Engineering success that will keep them in line
To top it all out in another 100 years time.

Amen

A GOURMET OCCASION; AN EDWARDIAN BANQUET BICENTENARY OF PAYNE & GUNTER, 1786–1986

Tallow Chandlers' Hall, 31 October 1986
Host: John Coomb

'Whenever the accent is on the elegant, stylish or even eccentric, Payne & Gunter have two centuries of experience to ensure a truly memorable occasion.'

John Coomb's party at Tallow Chandlers' Hall certainly measured up to that claim. He very kindly invited me to this gourmet session as I had known him while he was a Director of Ring & Brymer. He had joined them as an apprentice in 1949 after War Service in Combined Operations. After 30 years with Rings he joined Payne & Gunter to be their City Director. Royal appointments; High Society, West End, had really been Gunter's traditional background. Catering at top sporting and social events gave them an additional dimension.

John was able, by contrast, to concentrate on the highly competitive City catering market. The celebration included his commentary, course by course. Guests savoured that too as he is a connoisseur of both food and drink. The wines and menu are on pp. 141–2.

Graces on Sundry Occasions

GRACE

Bless us, O Lord, as at Tallows we dine
Enjoying John's food with appropriate wine
No need to multiply the loaves and fishes
But please do have a kindly care
For us and the gargantuan fare
Of Payne & Gunter's Edwardian dishes.

                                        Amen

WINES

Taittinger Brut Reserve

*

Rainwater Dry Madeira, Barbeito

*

Alsace Riesling Cuvée Frederic Emile 1981
F E Trimbach

*

Château Latour Saint Bonnet 1978
A C Medoc, Château Bottled

*

Veuve Clicquot Yellow Label

*

Santenay Saint-Michel 1979
Prosper Maufoux, Domaine Bottled

*

Hochheimer Konigin Victoria Berg
Riesling Spatlese 1983 Deinhard

*

Graham's Malvedos 1968

*

Château de Brives
Petite Champagne Cognac Prunier

MENU

Créme de Pois Nouveaux

*

Côtelette de Saumon à la Montpelier

*

Salmis de Faisan

Graces on Sundry Occasions

Sorbet de Champagne

*

Selle d'Agneau à la Portugaise
Légumes de Saison

*

Crêpe Alexandra

*

Café

TOASTMASTERS' GRACES

I asked Bernard Sullivan, Past President of the Society of London Toastmasters, who has gavelled most of my Graces, if he had one to offer:

> We who pray silence for other folks' graces
> Will shortly sit down to feed our own faces
> God bless our food and the guests at our side
> And thank you, dear Lord, for all you provide.
>
> Amen

Red-coated Toastmasters, he told me, 'should, in his opinion, be men who like people. They should be capable of persuading their fellow citizens to move from one room to another, sit down, stand up, etc . . . in quick time but without offence. They should have a good knowledge of English protocol, plenty of confidence in dealing with Dukes as well as Dustmen, coupled with the ability not to flap. They should have the sort of voice that fixes one's attention. (Some of us is good-looking too!).' Bernard has 'the lot'. I can always be relaxed when he is on duty as I know that everything will be under control including the unpredictable, temperamental microphones. He has become a good friend. I treasure a trophy which he gave me when I retired. Mounted on a plinth, his inscription reads: 'A genuine piece of Old London Bridge Stone, stolen at great price by a well known London Toastmaster on the night of the 19 September 1969 and presented to the Revd. Watson'.

All who have responded to his gavel were delighted when he was awarded the MBE in the Queen's Birthday Honours 1990.

Graces on Sundry Occasions

ANOTHER GRACE OF HIS

Bless us O Lord Divine
Who turned the water into wine
Have mercy on those foolish men
Who try to turn it back again.

                                                     Amen

GRACE

For heaped plates and brimming cup
And freedom from the washing up
Good Lord deliver us.

                                                     Amen

GRACE

For lamb that's old and lamb that's young
For lamb that's hot and lamb that's cold
For lamb that's tender and that's tough
We thank Thee, Lord, we've had enough.

                                                     Amen

GRACE

God of goodness, bless our food
Keep us in a pleasant mood
Bless the cook and all who serve us
And from indigestion do preserve us
If long speeches we'll endure
Give us first a good liqueur.

                                                     Amen

GRACE ATTRIBUTED TO SIR STEPHEN GASELEE

On china blue, my lobster red
Precedes my cutlet brown
Which with my salad green is sped
By yellow Chablis down
Lord if good living be no sin but innocent delight
Oh polarise these hues within
To one upeptic white.

                                                     Amen

Graces on Sundry Occasions

GRACE

For boiled and grilled
And fried and roast
Praise Father, Son and Holy Ghost.

                                                                       Amen

A BREAKFAST GRACE

For scrambled eggs and buttered toast
Praise Father, Son and Holy Ghost.

                                                                        Amen

A GRACE FOUND WRITTEN IN AN HOTEL BOOK

Grant me, Lord, the grace to see
How to render thanks to Thee
When Thy gifts are so mistreated
Meat, grown cold, has been reheated
Lettuce, limp and brown with time
Wilts in nameless yellow slime
While behind the scenes they toil
Frying chips in linseed oil
Cardboard pastry, rubber cream
Caramel, thy name blaspheme
Woolly biscuits, sweaty cheese
Save me Lord, from those and these
Though I shan't come here again
Grant me courage to complain.

                                                                      Amen

GRACE IN NAVAL MESS

Reporting to the President at the beginning of dinner, the Chief Steward said:
'No Chaplain present'
President: 'Thank God'.

                                                                      Amen

OF NAVAL BREVITY

On us and these
Thy blessing please

                                                                      Amen

Graces on Sundry Occasions

A VARIANT ON AN OFT-USED GRACE

For good food and good friends —
and the occasional enemy, thank God.

> Amen

A BUTLER'S GRACE

Benedictus Benedicanter

> Amen

A SPOONERISM

Sir James Miskin, recently Recorder of the City of London, who spoke more frequently almost after dinner than I said Grace before, constantly made me the butt of his humour at the beginning of a speech when we were on the same bill of fare. It was for a one-time spoonerism of which, he said, I was guilty . . . 'and keep us ever needful of the minds of others'.

BISHOP FLEMING'S GRACE

Bishop Lancelot Fleming, a wartime naval Chaplain, tutor of Trinity Hall, Cambridge and Bishop of Portsmouth, later became Bishop of Norwich. Both there and as Dean of Windsor he was very much the confidant of HRH The Duke of Edinburgh. Like the Duke, he was a 'doer of the word' and that was expressed in his Grace:

> O Lord grant that we may not be like porridge
> Stiff, stodgy and hard to stir
> But like cornflakes, crisp, fresh and ready to serve.

A GRACE FOR ALL OCCASIONS, WHATEVER THE
PARTICULAR EVENT; ENDING

. . . and may each one of us in our own way give thanks for our good fortune in being here tonight.

> Amen

HMS LONDON: LAUNCH ON THE CLYDE, 1984
LUNCH AT YARROWS

The Lord Mayor of London, the first Lady Lord Mayor, Dame Mary Donaldson was most appropriately invited to launch the new HMS

Graces on Sundry Occasions

London by Yarrow Shipbuilders on 27 October 1984. Although I was not her official Chaplain, she very kindly asked me to accompany her on this occasion, knowing what pleasure such a naval ceremony would give.

She had taken an interest in my activities ever since she had been a member of the Corporation interview panel who chose me from a shortlist of eight for appointment to St Lawrence Jewry. The return to the Clyde also gave me the chance to stay with Sir Eric and Lady Yarrow. It was in his old yard that the launch was to take place, but alas, since nationalisation, they were not on the official guest list. Such disappointment as they might have had was never mentioned while I feared that my visit might rub salt in the wound. It was a great joy to me to find him happily absorbed in his new firm of maritime scientific research, known as Yard, and to be invited to lunch with his Board. It so happened too that he was asked that day to become Chairman of the Clydesdale Bank. It was altogether a most happy visit during which they made time for me to see that fascinating accumulation of objets d'arts, the Burrell Collection.

After the successful launch in the presence of many shipbuilding, industrial and political VIPs; with all the bunting and the flag waving of the wives and families of those who had been involved in the building of this magnificent looking hull of a vessel, we adjourned for naval refreshment. I had said launching Prayers before the bottle of champagne had made its mark on the bows, and was then invited to say Grace at the celebratory Dinner:

GRACE

London is safely launched on the Clyde
How smoothly the Lord Mayor got her to glide
The spume and the spray
Lead us now, Lord, to pray
A blessing on all that's made Yarrow this day.

                                                                  Amen

ADDENDUM

St Lawrence Jewry was no sinecure in spite of my levity at the interview. We hardly ever had less than 1000 seated in church each week, though never on Sundays!

That pecular routine — a vicar unemployed on Sundays — amused an Alderman, Sir Charles Trinder, a ship owner and noted

Graces on Sundry Occasions

wit. He greatly approved of what was going on at St Lawrence Jewry but never missed an opportunity of having fun at my expense. 'I was listening to a lecture last night on unemployment', he said 'The speaker did a breakdown of the numbers: there were so many seasonally unemployed: so many transitionally unemployed: so many school-leavers: so many women unemployed. And then he said we are left with the hard core: the wholly unemployed . . .' 'Basil', he continued with that twinkle which alerted me to the double entendre that was coming, 'I could only think of you'.

LLOYDS: THE CHAIRMAN'S DINNER

Chairman 1980–1983 Peter Green

The Chairman entertains the Lord Mayor and civic dignitaries, and the chairmen of the principal institutions of the Financial City, to an annual dinner that has a unique character. It is very different in aura from Livery Dinners and other Civic Banquets. Guests are taken on arrival by young men to a particular area of the reception room to join the other invitees who will be dining at the same table. During those pre-dinner drinks one gets to know each of them sufficiently well to be able to indulge in general table talk later; rather than be limited, as so often is the case, to one's immediate neighbours. All are round tables seating twelve, and designated not by letters or numbers, but by a particular hue of sweet pea. The formal is delightfully blended with the easy personal relationships. I cannot remember what we ate or drank on the occasions that we were privileged to attend: but we always came away feeling that we had experienced the perfection of such entertainment.

Peter Green is caught up in the ramifications of our family life. From the letters he received on the death of his wife — Pammy — I had the honour of compiling a tribute to that remarkable lady in the Memorial Service which was held at St Lawrence Jewry. Our invitations to the Dinner came while he was Chairman.

> GRACE
> We've come, O Lord, from the East and the West
> To enjoy what your providence gives at its best
> Should the Lord Mayor remark to the good Peter Green
> On the wonders of Lime Street we've already seen

Graces on Sundry Occasions

He'd doubtless disarmingly say
In his usual modest, nonchalant way
'It's just to take the edge off your aching voids
That you come to dine with the Chairman of Lloyds'.

              Amen

LONDON TOURIST BOARD

Silver Jubilee Luncheon
The Mansion House in the presence of the Rt Hon the
 Lord Mayor and Lady Mayoress,
Wednesday 9 November 1988
Chairman: Sir Christopher Leaver KBE

GRACE

LTB
Ends its Silver Jubilee
In this lunch at the Mansion House
When they give thanks for our green and our pleasant
 land
Our heritage our silver sea and our sand
And, before taking McIver's fine wine
They feelingly ask a blessing divine
That what we eat will be free of the fever
And bring good cheer to us and Sir Christopher Leaver.

              Amen

The lunch was one of the first after a disastrous outbreak of salmonella poisoning was experienced at the City Lands Banquet.

Sir Christopher Leaver was Lord Mayor 1981–82 and became Chairman of the LTB in 1988. He is Chairman of Russel McIvers, wine merchant.

WAITANGI DAY

The New Zealand High Commission and members of the New Zealand Society in England celebrate their National Day on 6 February, Waitangi Day.

The festivities commemorate the signing of the Treaty in 1840 between the British and the Maori Chiefs of New Zealand. By it they ceded all their rights and powers of sovereignty to the British Monarch, while retaining their territorial rights and receiving protection.

Graces on Sundry Occasions

A large buffet lunch at the Bank of New Zealand gathers a party together who then attend an afternoon service at St Lawrence Jewry, followed by tea in Girdlers' Hall. A Banquet is held in the evening either in the River Room at the Savoy or at the Royal Lancaster where the walls expand to the numbers attending.

There is a human story behind the church and the festivities. Walter Besley, Rector of St Lawrence Jewry 1920–1935, went to New Zealand to be cured of TB. On his return, in gratitude, he made the ancilliary church premises available to the High Commission and for New Zealand nurses in London. He also suggested to the Worshipful Company of Girdlers, one of the Livery Companies attached to the church and within easy walking distance of it, that they might like to offer refreshments at the Hall after the annual commemorative service. Out of this has developed a relationship between the Company and the Society which now has many ramifications at national level. Among them, and of great potential, is an annual award of four scholarships, worth £10,000 each at Corpus Christi College, Cambridge.

It was the Rector's experience which led a City policeman, Bill Jordan, to emigrate to New Zealand. He soon entered politics there and returned to the UK as a member of Winston Churchill's wartime Commonwealth Cabinet.

The Master and Wardens of the Girdlers are always honoured guests at their Waitangi Banquet. Since the EC has discriminated against New Zealand imports, and set aside our established markets of the old Imperial Preference days, it has proved a patriotic and popular gesture for the Society to arrange a special shipment of New Zealand provisions for the occasion.

Banquet at the Royal Lancaster Hotel
Tuesday 6 February 1980
Chairman: Brian Shaw

>GRACE
>
>It's New Zealanders who gather and now stand to pray
>In honour, Lord, of our Waitangi Day
>So a blessing we ask ere we sit down to dine
>On our special victuals and good Kiwi wine
>Did Europe permit it we'd enjoy so much more
>Of the goodies we purchased in those days of yore
>That's a statement of fact

Graces on Sundry Occasions

Not lack of tact
And required to rhyme with . . . our Brian Shaw.

Amen

THE ROSS McWHIRTER FOUNDATION AND FREEDOM ASSOCIATION DINNERS

Ross McWhirter was shot down at the front door of his home in Enfield on 27 November 1975 by two IRA gunmen. He was murdered because, after his friend Professor Gordon Hamilton-Fairley the cancer expert, had been blown up by an IRA bomb, he tried to get the Home Office to introduce bounties for information leading to convictions. The Home Office do so now, but then Ross had to organise his own £50,000 bounty through private enterprise. His courage in doing so cost him his life at the hand of the 'Active Service Unit', the last known and fifth member of which was convicted and received a life sentence in February 1988.

His twin brother, Norris, encouraged by Dr (the Rt Hon Sir) Rhodes Boyson and Ralph (Lord) Harris, set up a Foundation to honour his memory, as a courageous champion of Freedom under the Law.

The declared aim of the Foundation:

'To promote the mental and moral improvement of the public in the principles and practice of good citizenship, and in particular as to the exercise of personal courage both in a moral and physical context as an example to others.'

Each year awards are made at an annual dinner to those who are adjudged to have shown exceptional courage. The awards are presented and citations read by Rosemary, (now Mrs Mostyn) Ross's widow. Among previous winners are Vladimir Bukovsky; George Ward (Grunwick); Raoul Wallenberg (in absentia); Eddy Shah; Fr Gleb Yakunin. Many, with less famous names, have been honoured. Of the five awards made in 1988, that of Mrs Dawn Cook, reads:

'She was a postal clerk of Bristol whose alertness, persistence and courage in May and June 1986 resulted in the arrest and conviction of two bank robbers. In addition to alerting police about the gang 16 days before they struck, she endeavoured to block their get-away vehicle with her own car and gave chase while vigorously sounding her horn. Subsequent harassment drove her to emigrate.'

At the Dinner a Memorial Address is given. The fifteenth such occasion was held at Middle Temple Hall on Tuesday 3 November

Graces on Sundry Occasions

1992 when Lord Weatherill, Speaker of the House of Commons 1983–1992 proposed the toast. Lord Harris of High Cross is a frequent speaker on these occasions.

He was Chairman of the Institute of Economic Affairs and the first economist to be ennobled by Mrs Thatcher for his part in imbuing her with the virtues of the market economy and of private enterprise. He gave her a crusading conviction to defeat the post-war addiction to Socialism in the trendy Left, and the middle-of-the-road-ism — 'the wets' — of her own party.

> GRACE
>
> The years pass but the memory does not fade
> For each of us lives something of the Freedom Ross has made
> The Awards list lengthens
> People's courage yearly strengthens
> Citations too sound even more like fables
> Lord, bless thy gifts and the fellowship of our tables.
>
> Amen

I have said Grace on most occasions during the 15 years of the Foundation; the first:

> GRACE
>
> For all who meet in affectionate memory of Ross,
> we ask, O Lord, a continuing trust in the Freedom
> enshrined in our Law and, for a blessing on
> the strengthening fellowship of our table, that we may
> courageously pursue the noble idea to which he inspired
> us.
>
> Amen

Anniversary Dinner at Goldsmiths' Hall, March 1985

> GRACE
>
> Inspire, O Lord, all who gather here in memory of Ross and strengthen our Foundation in his honour. May we act with his courage when we know that the freedom and liberties of others are endangered. As we share these gifts of food and wine in fellowship, bless them to our use and ourselves to thy service in the lives of the oppressed.
>
> Amen

Graces on Sundry Occasions

Ross had been a great help to me at St Lawrence Jewry where he took a keen interest in what I was trying to do through my Wednesday rostrum. His editorship of the *Guinness Book of Records* seemed to give him access to everyone. He was able to recommend speakers for courses, approaching them often on my behalf.

I serve on the Council of the Freedom Association chaired by Norris.

GRACE AT THE ANNUAL DINNER OF THE ASSOCIATION

O God
For they bounty we thank thee
For those in hunger: we pray thee
For the oppressed: their enduring courage, we ask thee
For our Freedom: it is high praise we give thee
For these and all thy gracious gifts we bless thee.

Amen

The Freedom Association Dinner at the time of the Liberation of Eastern Europe.
Principal speaker: The Rt Hon Norman Tebbitt MP

GRACE

We celebrate each year the champions of men's freedom
The Norman Tebbitts and those who extend that spiritual Kingdom
So tonight, as we dine,
We ask a blessing divine
Not just on the gracious gifts of the table
But on Europe's other brave spirits who 're now making Freedom no fable.

Amen

Annual Commemoration Dinner:
The Ross McWhirter Foundation,
Middle Temple Hall, 11 April 1989

GRACE

We need our heroes and champions of Freedom
Those who fight for the Laws that uphold our Kingdom
Here where we worship that ideal in this Temple
We uphold Ross in such honour as makes tyrants tremble

Graces on Sundry Occasions

So we ask now, O Lord, a blessing divine
As in the fellowship of memory we sit down to dine.

                                                                         Amen

Ross McWhirter's Memorial Dinner
Middle Temple Hall, 6 November 1990

GRACE

We thank thee, Lord, that year on year as we remember Ross
We're kept aware that Freedom's price is what we call a cross
It's a special blessing that we pray on our Dinner here tonight
That strengthened by its friendships we'll carry on that fight.

                                                                         Amen

Ross McWhirter Foundation
Dinner at Middle Temple Hall, 29 October 1991
Chairman: The Rt Hon Lord Rippon of Hexham

GRACE

We're not all made of the same mettle as Ross
But we find, dining together, gets the good from the dross
Our spirits are raised by courageous deeds done
And we delight in the golden opinions people have won
It's an evening for thoughts, and there's good food and wine
All we ask is your blessing, Lord, as we now sit down to dine.

                                                                         Amen

The Memorial Address was given by Field Marshal the Rt Hon Lord Bramall, KG, GCB, HM Lord Lieutenant of Greater London.

Graces on Sundry Occasions

RENDEL PALMER AND TRITTON

150th Anniversary Banquet at Guildhall, 23 November 1988
Chairman: Robert Wharton

GRACE

Up in the gallery are Gog and Magog
On this north wall Winston, Nelson and Pitt
Tonight in Guildhall among our nation's heroes
We are privileged to sit
And we too bring to the table
A Thames-side saga that reads more like a fable
Which Rendel Palmer and Tritton have told
While becoming 150 years old
So now before we sit down to dine
We ask a blessing divine
That we'll enjoy all that's to come and have lots of fun
And still get home safely when the evening is done.

Amen

Note

Rendel Palmer and Tritton are a firm of consulting and design engineers, noted particularly for their work along the Thames.

CITY OF LONDON SPECIAL CONSTABULARY

Annual Dinner: Whitbreads 1984

St Lawrence Jewry being a church only and not a parish, meant that there were no on-the-site hands to help with all the odd jobs. I soon found that, with Wood Street Police Station within one hundred yards, I had no need to worry. Police rallied round to support on and off duty. They always checked on the church doors at night as they passed. Subsequent 'phone calls were not always popular at the vicarage! They stood by to give protection when VIPs came to speak on Wednesdays. They helped to rig Christmas trees and knew everyone who could fix anything. I was to find myself one of them in return — as a Special. Kitted out in a uniform, I've been on the beat — marched down Cheapside: paraded for inspection at Mansion House and always, but always, been present at the Annual Dinner, recently held at Whitbreads (*vide:* Guildhall). I was never happier with any group of men and cherish a well engraved port decanter as a token of those friendships.

Graces on Sundry Occasions

The Commandant always brought distinguished guests. The only scrap of paper which I can find with Graces that I used on these occasions refers to the time when H E the Cardinal Archbishop of Westminster honoured us.

Archbishop Basil Hume is good at getting around the City and everyone feels the better for his presence. On the increasing occasions that we met I found a close affinity and an easy encounter. Though he queried the theology he took no exception to the spirit of the Grace, and sat down to the goodwill of the Force, and Basil its Chaplain.

> GRACE
> There were Cappadocian Fathers called Basil
> Who, with the Police of their day,
> One can safely say
> Never had a night on the razzle
> But its different here where we both bid you pray
> That the Lord will be good
> Looking after us and the food
> That neither get done to a frazzle.
>
> Amen

A farewell occasion: Frank Ralfe, Chief Commandant

'On behalf of all the Special Constabulary, through three Commandants and four Commissioners, may I thank you for being our Chaplain and for the unique and much appreciated graces that you have said for us at the Annual Dinners over the past sixteen years.

We wish you and Mrs Watson many years of good health and happiness in your new home at Greenwich and trust that, as a Life Member of the Wakefield Mess, you will return to see us and refresh the parts that the Thames Water Authority cannot reach.

I commend to you:

> 'A SPECIAL'S LAMENT'
> 'No meal of ours will be the same again
> Without those resonant and lofty tones.
> Without the mint of Basil to spice the food,
> A tasteless future looks us in the face,
> Without our Chaplain's presence,
> Known not for his airs — but for his grace.'

'There were Cappadocian Fathers called Basil.'
Photograph by Courtesy of Universal Pictorial Press.

Graces on Sundry Occasions

WOMEN'S NATIONAL
CANCER CONTROL CAMPAIGN

Judith Chalmers set up the Appeals Committee for WNCCC in 1972. Her husband, Neil Durden-Smith was a cadet in the Training Cruiser shortly after the War while I was Chaplain. On a number of occasions, I have had the pleasure of taking part in Judith's fund-raising activities, at lunch in the Grosvenor House Hotel.

Assisted by Barbara Upsdell, she raised over £40,000 in 1988 in support of an organisation that was founded in 1964 in the borough of Stoke Newington. The local initiative was soon lifted up into the national sphere when it was realised how important was the early detection and prevention of cervical cancer. The campaign was to become a vital source of health education in the field of women's cancer generally, and in particular of breast cancer and the smear test. It now finances five mobile clinics and screens approximately 40,000 women every year, though sadly there were 2000 unnecessary deaths from cervical cancer last year. If detection had been early enough, a large proportion of the 14,000 women who died of breast cancer could have been saved.

It is impossible to over-emphasise the gratitude of the great number of women who have benefited. The value of the campaign has been recognised by the frequent attendance of Royalty at fund raising occasions, like the annual Spring luncheon held at either the Grosvenor House or the Hilton Hotel. Sponsorship and support comes from nearly every High Street firm and organisation. Celebrities from stage, screen and sport are enthusiastic in their vociferous support of Judith on the working lunch platform as she charms the money out of their pockets.

The campaign depends on such fund raising: it is not backed up by a Marie Curie Foundation or an Imperial Research Fund. It is on its own. I am always fascinated and enthused by the practical good will stirred up by such occasions.

I have in mind the first time at the Grosvenor House Hotel that we were all to be seated in the great Ballroom at round tables for twelve. Somewhat naturally there is always a preponderance of women for this lunch. Without male escorts, anxious to get them properly seated, they continue to chatter theatrically, even when the Toastmaster is trying to issue instructions on how to get to their places. Reading a table plan and working out the left hand side of the room from the right

Graces on Sundry Occasions

is also considered to be of secondary importance to their convivial greeting of friends.

Greetings among show-biz personalities, moreover, tend to be generously worded and time consuming. So it was twenty minutes between the lunch call and the moment that over 1000 of us found our places and were gavelled for Grace. That was the moment when I chose to say that it seemed a chance to make up some of the leeway.

GRACE

There are times when two words are better than ten
Tuck in, Amen.

Peterborough reported the Grace in his column in the Daily Telegraph. That brought in several hundred pounds as it reminded a number of absentees of the good cause they might have been supporting. Many sent Judith Chalmers their conscience money.

On another occasion at the Hilton, I said something by way of preamble to a Grace attributed to Bishop Lancelot Fleming. It was to the effect that all Charities flourish when everyone involved is evangelical about the cause and does not leave the work to the organiser alone.

GRACE

O Lord, grant that we may not be like
Porridge, stiff, stodgy and hard to stir; but
like cornflakes, crisp, fresh and ready to serve.

Amen

GRACE AT THE GROSVENOR HOUSE HOTEL, MARCH 1990

It was Mothering Sunday yesterday and we all gave our praise
To the Church and the Homes in which we were raised
On a love that gave strength to our lives.
And today it's a blessing we pray
Not just on our table
But on what this campaign makes us able
To do for our young would-be wives.

Amen

Graces on Sundry Occasions

THE ROYAL SOCIETY OF ST GEORGE
CITY OF LONDON BRANCH

The City of London Branch of the Royal Society of St George has a membership of 1160. Members usually hold a Christmas banquet at the Mansion House which the Lord Mayor attends. The great occasion of the year is, of course, St George's Day. Though he is no longer venerated in the Church's calendar, 23 April (as well as being Shakespeare's birthday) is still nationally observed, somewhat quietly, in his honour. The Society make much of it. Only Guildhall in the City is a large enough (Livery) Hall to seat the 600 who attend on this occasion. Even for the Christmas banquet, there is often a waiting list of more than a hundred, whatever the price of the ticket.

The other venue is Whitbreads. Until it was recently moved to the London Museum the Lord Mayor's coach was kept on their premises and three pairs of their famous shires still pull it through the streets of the City for the Lord Mayor's Show. They are a visible reminder of the firm which Samuel Whitbread founded in 1749 and housed in splendid Georgian industrial buildings. Whitbreads only ceased to brew their ales there at the heart of the City in 1976.

As part of the recent extensive Chiswell Street redevelopment, the premises were then converted to be further socially useful. Out of it came, among other facilities, the great Banqueting Hall known as the Porter Tun Room. So called because it could hold over a million and a half pints of Porter at a time — porter being a malt liquor similar to stout which Whitbreads did much to popularise in the mid-eighteenth century. Its unsupported king-post timber roof, the second largest in Europe, and its general spaciousness, give it an atmosphere which the diners in white ties, button holed and corsaged with the Red Rose of England, soon make festive on St George's night. In the course of the banquet, the roast beef of England is ceremonially paraded, usually escorted by the drums and piccolo of the Royal Marines or the Corps of Drums of the Honourable Artillery Company.

After the Chairman has pronounced his approval of the beef and commended it to the diners for their enjoyment he takes ale, now brewed elsewhere, with the head chef and his assistants. This is a moment of high drama. It was on St George's Day 1987, W B Fraser being Chairman, that I offered Grace in this assembly of patriots:

Graces on Sundry Occasions

GRACE

St George for England cried Harry
And we in this Porter Tun Room
Re-echo that cry
Till its heard up on high
And we're blessed from the womb to the tomb.
For the rest — of the bard I'll be brief
So we enjoy our sweet tasting beef
And chatter away on the friendships we forge
In making England stiffly to stand for St George.
                                                Amen

('stiffly to stand' for St George — *vide* 2 Esdras Chapter 2 v47)

On other occasions a standard form of Grace, composed by the Rt Revd. E J K Roberts, sometime Lord Bishop of Ely, is used:

GRACE

God save the Queen and prosper the Royal Society
of St George, and bless His gifts of food and
drink to our benefit and enjoyment, that we
may faithfully serve England for God and for St George.
                                                Amen

The Objects of the Society

There are other social and cultural events in the course of the Society's year: all designed to further the objects of the Society:
• To foster the love of England and to strengthen England and the commonwealth by spreading the knowlege of English history, traditions and ideals.
• To keep fresh the memory of those in all walks of life who have served England or the Commonwealth in the past, in order to inspire leadership in future.
• To combat all activities likely to undermine the strength of England or the Commonwealth.
• To further English interests everywhere, to ensure that St George's Day is properly celebrated and to provide focal points all the world over where English men and women may gather together.
    It was such rarely held sentiments in the permissive, satirical, disestablishment 'sixties' which provoked the formation of the Society.

Graces on Sundry Occasions

The grant of the Royal Charter, its 25th anniversary, will be observed in 1988 with a service of Thanksgiving in St Lawrence Jewry, the Church of the Corporation of London. Very characteristic of the Society to do so. It sponsored a previous service held to mark the 40th anniversary of VE Day and asked that my sermon should be printed.

Leading up to this there have been significant national occasions which the Chairman, John Minshull-Fogg, has arranged for the Society to celebrate in his year: the Bicentenary of MCC and the quatercentenary of the Armada. At the dinner, held in the Lord's Banqueting Suite on 10 September 1987, I arranged, through the Chairman, that the Toastmaster would gavel only, leaving me to announce:-

> GRACE — WG — AND A N OTHER
> Before we raise our knives and forks
> And enjoy what comes from well drawn corks
> Or hear great talk of cricket's fame
> By those who play the English game
> Let's bless and praise our Lord Divine
> For his good gifts of food and wine.
>
> Amen

G Hubert Doggart, Treasurer of the MCC and Chairman of the Bicentennial Committee, in responding for the guests made a most approving reference to the Grace and requested a copy for the annals.

Other speakers included the Hon Peter Brooke MP, Paymaster General, H M Treasury who proposed the toast to the MCC and cricket, to which J J Warr, President Designate of the MCC replied. Colin Cowdrey, who was recovering from open heart surgery, sent apologies and best wishes for the evening. The Chairman, a cricket correspondent of the *Daily Telegraph* for many years, as he reflected on those magical names in proposing the toast to England and St George, was able to announce a gift of £2,000 towards coaching the not-so-privileged young at Lord's. The Society exists for more than wineing and dining!

Where better could the Society have held the Armada Dinner, celebrating the quater-centenary of the defeat of the Spanish, than in the Middle Temple Hall where Sir Francis Drake was a bencher and where there is a table, called 'the Cupboard' made out of timber which he presented from the Golden Hind.

Hearts of oak, nay whole trees, possibly 800/900 years old, form the eight principal floor joists of the Hall. They are about 18x13 inches

Graces on Sundry Occasions

thick and 44 feet long. There are also eight double hammer beam roof trusses. In all it is some 100 feet long by 40 wide and from floor to apex it is 59 feet.

The Hall dates from the same period as the Armada and survived both the Great First and Second World War. In the magnificence of its Tudor atmosphere the Society had a feeling of being an authentic part of our maritime and legal history on this privileged occasion.

GRACE

Howard, Grenville, Raleigh, Drake
Here's to the bold and free
Hawkins, Frobisher, Borough and Blake
Hail to the Kings of the sea
Englishmen all we're proud to be
Celebrating the Armada victory
In this Temple Hall
Which keeps us in thrall
To a table timbered from the Golden Hind
Where Shakespeare's *Twelfth Night* is brought to mind
Played in the presence of the Virgin Queen
Lord bless us all, in this patriot's scene.

Amen

With acknowledgements to Henry Newbolt.

(On 2 February 1601, *Twelfth Night* was played probably with William Shakespeare himself in the cast, and possibly in the presence of the Queen who frequently visited the Hall).

Speakers included Admiral Sir Simon Cassels KCB, CBE, Chairman of the Sir Francis Drake Heritage Appeal from Buckland Abbey, Drake's old home, where his Drum is housed. Also, significantly too, Admiral Sir Nicholas Hunt KCB, MVO, recently Commander in Chief, Fleet.

When I went to my place after saying Grace, the head Bench Butler, M Stanley Waring, attended to me and recited the Graces traditionally used in the Hall. He later, very kindly, sent me a copy.

GRACE BEFORE MEAT

The eyes of all things look up and
put their trust in Thee, O Lord:
Thou givest them their Meat in
due season; Thou openest Thine
hand, and fillest with Thy blessing

every living thing. Good Lord,
bless us and these Thy good gifts
which we receive of Thy bounteous
liberality, through Jesus Christ
Our Lord.

Amen

GRACE AFTER MEAT

Glory, honour, and praise be given to
thee, O Lord, who dost feed us from our
tender age, and givest sustenance to
every living thing. Replenish our
hearts with joy and gladness, that we,
having sufficient, may be rich and
plentiful in all good works, through
Jesus Christ our Lord. God save his
Church, the Queen, all the Royal Family,
and this Realm: God send us peace and
truth in Christ our Lord.

Amen

Another national occasion which was observed by the City of London Branch for the first time, on the initiative of the Chairman, John Minshull-Fogg, was the Trafalgar Dinner, held on 21 October 1987 at the Waldorf Hotel.

After the Toastmaster had gavelled silence for Grace: 'With the Chairman's permission before I offer the traditional Grace used in the Navy and attributed to Nelson, I quote the prayer which he wrote on the eve of the battle which we commemorate tonight:

'May the great God whom I worship grant to my country, and for the benefit of Europe in general, a great and glorious victory, and may no misconduct in the British Fleet after battle tarnish it. For myself individually, I commit myself to him who made me and the just cause which is given me to defend. Amen. Amen. Amen.

God save the Queen: bless our victuals and make us thankful. Amen'.

The toast of the evening — the Immortal Memory — was proposed by Admiral Sir Raymond Lygo KCB, Chief Executive, British Aerospace plc. Raymond had been a Lieutenant in the Fleet Air Arm when I was Chaplain at Culdrose. I invited Bryan Green, the Evangelist who had greatly influenced me at Cambridge, to conduct a mission to the

Graces on Sundry Occasions

station. As Bryan Green arrived, Ray Lygo took his flight in formation over the airfield in the form of a Cross. *In hoc signo vinces.* It was that sign which the Emperor Constantine saw in the sky leading him on to victory over the Huns at the battle of the Milvian Bridge in 312. Christianity thereby became a permitted, no longer persecuted, religion of the Roman Empire. It was an inspiring speech on the nature of Christian virtues, as Englishmen understand them, which members of the Society heard that evening to give them hope in our country's future.

The Christmas Banquet, Thursday 17 December
Held at Mansion House in the presence of the Lord Mayor,
  Alderman Sir Greville Spratt GBE TD DL.

The Governor of the Bank of England, the Rt Hon Robin Leigh-Pemberton responded to the toast of the guests proposed by Bernard Morgan, the President.

'England and St George', the toast of the evening, was proposed by Field Marshal the Lord Bramall GCB OBE MC JP, Her Majesty's Lord-Lieutenant of Greater London.

> GRACE
>
> In the festive season of peace and goodwill
> When Mansion House warms, though the evening be chill
> And we of St George on this night of the year
> Rejoice in our Christmas and all its good cheer
> We pray, Lord, a blessing on all those in need
> So that England keeps faith in word and in deed.
>
> Amen

St George's Day Celebration Banquet at Guildhall
23 April 1988
Chairman: John Minshull-Fogg

This banquet marked the end of the Chairman's exceptionally patriotic year. The quotation which he chose for this menu card was from Winston Churchill:

'There is a forgotten nay almost forbidden word, which means more to me than any other. That word is England. Once we flaunted

Graces on Sundry Occasions

it in the face of the whole world like a banner. It was a word of power. But today we are scarcely allowed to mention the name of our country. I want to revive the grand old name of Englishmen!'

Guildhall Banquet, St George's Day, 1989

GRACE

In the gallery are Gog and Magog
Down there, Winston, Nelson and Pitt
Among our nation's heroes in Guildhall we're now privileged to sit
And we're here to keep St George, to honour Zeebrugge and the Bard
Alas to say farewell to John and Meg who've always worked so hard
To keep us ever merry in our proud thoughts of England
Bless them and us, O Lord, with all the bounty of our green and pleasant land.

Amen

Christmas Banquet, 19 December 1990

GRACE

St George courageously served his Lord
As we sit down now to our English board
We spare more than a thought for our fighting men
That the spirit of Christmas will not elude them.

Amen

Trafalgar Night Dinner, 22 October 1990
Held at Grosvenor House at the time of the Gulf crisis
Guest of Honour: Admiral Sir Julian Oswald GCB ADC, First Sea Lord

GRACE

'England expects' — and even press-ganged sailors cheered that day
And we now in their wake, 'gainst another tyrant proudly lead the way
Here assembled by our saintly patron the courageous George

Graces on Sundry Occasions

We ask a blessing, Lord, as patriotic links of fellowship we forge
To keep us ever resolute as you know who would say,
And on our victuals, good English fare, a bounteous Grace we pray.

                                                    Amen

Note
Resolute was a frequently used rallying word of Mrs Thatcher.

A GRACE FOR BANQUET OCCASIONS BY ALL BRANCHES

God be praised
Who has given us a green and pleasant land and set it, as Freedom's fortress, in a silver sea; who has also bred in us such a pride as makes us rejoice in our royal and ancient traditions.
Bless now, O Lord, these further gifts to our present use that the friendships of our table may strengthen us with the courage of St George to serve England faithfully and uphold her noble cause.

                                                    Amen

Guildhall, 22 April 1991

GRACE

On St George's Day
Englishmen pray
For our green and pleasant land
Tonight
May our Roast Beef prove tender
And guests of each gender
Enjoy talk as well as the band.

                                                    Amen

Grosvenor House, Trafalgar Dinner, Monday 21 October 1991

GRACE

On the eve of Trafalgar that signal was sent
What Nelson said about sailors he nationally meant
Do our duty
To God and our country

Graces on Sundry Occasions

Then 'England expects' his blessing divine
On victorious living — and the pleasures of wine.

Amen

St George's Christmas Banquet
Chartered Accountants' Hall, 19 December 1991

GRACE

Our Christmas banquet we hold in a different venue tonight
Its seasonal traditions here to shed their love and their light
Making us, like St George, want to honour our Lord
So we ask him to bless our most promising board
That He'll also keep us mindful of those in need
Merry and happy in our every Christmassy deed.

Amen

Guildhall Banquet, 22 April 1992

GRACE

We're not just a State but a Nation
People for whom Patriotism is always in fashion
We've got Gog and Magog safely keeping an eye
While soon the praises of roast beef will rise up on high
We ask a blessing, O Lord, on the friendships we forge
As we dine together to honour St George.

Amen

Grosvenor House, Trafalgar Night Dinner,
23 October 1992

GRACE

What a victory it would be for all we stand
If the Admiral atop his column at the end of the Strand
Could at last bequeath us his Trafalgar day
To replace that very un English occasion in May
We of St George pray such an outcome dear Lord
As well as your blessing on our evening's board.

Amen

Graces on Sundry Occasions

The Royal Society of St George
41st Anniversary Accession Dinner
Chairman: George R A Andrews, Esq.
5 February 1993

>GRACE
>
>Annus horribilis — plus one
>Better years will surely come
>For dragons can be slain
>St George our loyalty sustain
>Lord bless us and these gifts supreme
>May England still rejoice with our happier Queen.

THE VARIETY CLUB OF GREAT BRITAIN

'The greatest children's charity in the world'

Chief Barker, Harry Goodman
Lunch in Guildhall, 6 May 1987

>GRACE
>
>We're in company with Gog and Magog
>With Winston, Nelson and Pitt
>Among our nation's heroes in Guildhall we're now privileged to sit
>And the Variety Club of Great Britain
>Who do so much for children who're smitten
>Ask a blessing divine
>On their latest Life Line
>And Grace on their food and their wine.
>
>   Amen

One of the perks of saying Grace from behind the chair is that one frequently gets a word with the Chairman. 'I was talking to Rod only twenty minutes ago' said Harry Goodman. 'He's doing a great job.' Rod, our son, is Group Treasurer to Intasun, his travel firm in the International Leisure Group. The City is a small place: 'a square mile' by description: a human sized area where business can be done eyeball to eyeball and certainly a place, in pre Big Bang days, where much of its market strength came from knowledge of each other acquired not least through meeting socially on formal and other occasions.

Graces on Sundry Occasions

Established in October 1949, the Variety Club of Great Britain works exclusively to aid handicapped and deprived children throughout the UK regardless of their race, colour, creed and background. In this time it has raised and distributed almost £50 million to the benefit of children in hospitals, orphanages, residential homes, centres for the mentally and physically afflicted and individual families in distressed circumstances. The work covers the entire spectrum of child welfare.

When clubs of this nature come to celebrate their occasions they bring with them an enrichment of the life that has made Guildhall so much more than a building, and the Square Mile a Living City.

Appendixes and Epilogue

Appendixes

THE ROYAL NAVAL COLLEGE CHAPEL GREENWICH SERMON PREACHED ON 11 JUNE 1989 BY THE REVD. BASIL WATSON — (CHAPLAIN 1952–55)

My task this morning is to preach to you: your task is to listen to me! If, as they say, you should finish your task before I do, I crave a little further indulgence. Some of you appreciate that preaching from this pulpit is an activity which is close to my heart, and that I may want to bang on a little. I may even get near to that 20-minute limit which I used to set myself in my second incarnation here in 1968–70. By then I had been a preacher in the States on a number of occasions. Preaching is a different scene over there. On one of my early occasions a minister admonished me: 'Don't forget', he said, 'we're paying you 100 dollars for this, so we don't want any of your little ten minute so-called sermons here'. You have now been warned.

What gives me such pleasure in asking for your indulgence is the privilege of being able to speak about this Chapel in its 200th anniversary year, especially of that period in its history in which I had a hand 34 years ago — almost to the day. It was on the 21 June 1955, to be precise, when Archbishop Geoffrey Fisher, in the presence of the Queen Mother, rededicated the Chapel after its three years of restoration. He preached on that occasion, as I do now, on the costliness of religion; 'the best results of any venture in life are achieved at cost: at somebody's cost: best if it's at your own'. His was an impromptu sermon because I gave him the essence of it in the Vestry minutes only before we left to process into Church. I showed him from the Vestry what the workmen had done in excess of duty: at cost to themselves. He liked it. He repeated it up here in the pulpit. It registered.

What I had done, in fact, was to call his attention to the ceiling in the Memorial Chapel. Most of you will never have seen that. It is in the spacious area behind the Picture — an area that corresponds to the Upper Hall in that rather inferior building opposite, the Painted Hall! Within that area in Wren's Chapel, was the apse housing the High

Appendixes

Altar. As part of the restoration work I had turned part of the same area into a Requiem Chapel, gathering into it the plaques, memorials and brasses from the pre-War Chapel which had acquired frames of polish from years of sailors' attention. We wanted none of that on the new paint; besides, it was the appropriate place for these to be.

Naturally, I had wanted to make something special of that Chapel as a working repository of grateful memories. It had an already enriched plaster ceiling: but nothing as elaborate at this, though it had a certain distinction which I thought merited painting. It was not a big job but it did require skilled hands to do it.

Came the morning when I got my disappointment about it: the Ministry of Works regretted that they could not find the extra money for work which few could see. Downcast, I climbed the various flights of ladders which took me to the platform from which the painters worked on the ceiling — there were 33 of them who worked for nine months on it. I went up there almost daily, getting to know them. On this particular occasion I shared my sadness with them: and I'm sure that you realise that such a phrase is a euphemism for saying what I really felt. Later in the morning, the Foreman of Works came into my office to tell me that the painters had been talking during the tea break. They'd agreed that as the following Friday was Good Friday, a public holiday in those days, they'd like to give it to the Church: they'd come in and paint the ceiling. Marvellous, wasn't it? I was overwhelmed: so was the Archbishop when I told him. That's why he took their deed as the theme for his sermon. I watched the delighted smile grow on the face of the Queen Mother: the painters themselves were obviously pleased and even the Minister of Works, Nigel Birch at the time, somewhat shame-faced to begin with, became approving of his work force. The Archbishop had made his point: 'the best results in life are achieved at cost to oneself'. I reiterate that now and go on to make it explicit in a text: 'Whosoever does not bear his cross and come after me, cannot be my disciple'. St Luke, Chapter 14, v. 27.

I take a text as I want to assert that I'm preaching religion not talking architecture, though it may seem like it. It's in the theology of the restoration that I want to interest you: to take you behind what we architecturally did in 1952–5 to what it means for us today. Basically, I wanted to put an altar into the religion of the Chapel, to make the sacrifice of Christ the heart of our Faith, to give a celebration of Holy Communion its rightful place in our worship. That meant, first of all, pulling this pulpit away from the head and centre of the aisle, where

Appendixes

it stood when I came, to this position. Huge and magnificent as it is, I had no wish to belittle it: but I wanted an altar, equally large and impressive to balance it in its rightful place. In the Church of England it is by the altar at the focal point of a church, and by the pulpit to one side pointing to its significance, that we proclaim the Sovereignty of God in the Sacrifice of Christ. It is by Word and Sacrament that our spiritual life is sustained: by Bible reading and preaching, as well as Holy Communion. Both, the two together, lead us with authority to worship God and offer him the service of our love, of our lives.

Billy Graham is rightly saying, as on previous crusades, 'the Bible says: the Bible says' and he expects people to go forward and get enrolled in some form of Sacramental, Sacrificial Life. Word and Sacrament. Pulpit and Altar: the meaning of the two together, in emphasis and balance, was the point of the 1952–5 restoration. I wasn't interested in just restoring and painting, but in making the Chapel able to speak for itself for what it stood for, as far as the Church of England was concerned, in the life of the College, indeed in the life of the Navy. One day when Sir Christopher Wren was looking at St Paul's from the South Bank as it neared completion a voice at his side said 'And what will it do, Mr Architect: what will it do?'. Buildings, at their best, should proclaim their purpose. I wanted the Chapel by its layout to reassert its purpose: to be 'liturgical' in technical language: to proclaim its Eternal Gospel so that the Navy of my day could see the Faith expressed in all this magnificence and know the deeper meaning and certain cost of being on Active Service.

David Eccles (now Lord) was then Minister of Works and very sympathetic to what I was intending. He was a good High Churchman, as people used to be labelled, much as the yardstick today is whether you're for or against women priests or 1662. He understood that I wanted an altar and could see that it meant doing something about the Picture. Getting rid of it, in fact. So far so good. I then felt emboldened to say that I thought we could finance what I had in mind by selling the Picture to the Americans. Whatever intrinsic value it might have would be enhanced in value because its painter, Benjamin West, was the only American ever to be President of the Royal Academy. 'Wait a minute, parson', he said, 'it's not worth putting my political career at risk by selling yet another treasure across the Atlantic'. 'Seriously though' he said, 'you have to accept the Chapel as it is and it's no longer Wren's. Wren's structure yes, but decorated in the Adams

Appendixes

brothers style by "Athenian" Stewart. More importantly, it also reflects the Wesleyan movement which by 1789 had affected the whole Church with its emphasis on preaching and the pulpit. This is no exception — you'll have to keep that'. There was nothing one could quarrel with there: he was right historically. However, he appreciated that I wanted to be able to use it according to the Prayer Book as we understood it. We reached a working compromise, in approved fashion. I was to say nothing more about removing the Picture and consturcting an apse for an altar — and accept the Picture too in its own right as an appropriate symbol for the Pensioners (safely after shipwreck) for whom, of course, the College (Asylum/Hospital) was originally provided. Having got the pulpit to this position I could be free otherwise to do what I could to establish an Altar.

What then passed for an Altar was little more than a domestic semi-circular side table. If you look at it carefully you'll see that we lengthened it by a yard and gave it an extra foot in depth. We surrounded it by that delicate and beautifully restored wrought iron communion rail which had at some time been removed and was in pieces in the dome among other rejected furnishings. The bases with the swags which you see were up there too. When he saw them, Professor Sir Albert Richardson, President then of the Royal Academy, immediately saw a significant purpose for them. He was working on the restoration of the local church, St Alfege. Greenwich was still then largely derelict and, hard though it is now to believe it, without restaurants. I had the good fortune as a result to be able to invite him to lunch in the Painted Hall on his monthly visits. He used to come into the Chapel afterwards and cast an eye and comment on progress. On one such occasion he suggested the use of the bases so as to have a tromp d'oeil effect of an apse in front of, rather than behind the Altar. We cannibalised six into four bases. On two we placed flower vase stands and on the other two, copying the stem of the original lectern, we made the standard candelabra. They were then placed to outline a semi-circular pattern around the Altar. When they were gold-leafed and antiqued, as they say in the trade, to the texture of the arresting gilt frame of the Picture, they formed a setting for the Altar greater and more important than the pulpit. The bases were never meant to be individually eye-catching as pieces but to be all of a piece with the east end. Alas, the flower vase stands have been removed to the vestibule and the meaning of the symmetry has been lost, especially as it has all been so gaudily gilded.

Appendixes

At the heart of it all we commissioned a very special cross and candlesticks: as big and impressive as the extended Altar could carry. They were the work of Leslie Durbin, the leading silversmith of the period. He had just completed the ceremonial Sword of Stalingrad. It was fitting that his next piece of silver should be beaten not into a ploughshare but into the infinitely better symbol: the Cross. It was to cost us £5,000. In 1954 that wasn't peanuts. I asked a relative on Lloyds if they'd help us raise the money by starting the subscription list with £500. 'You'll never get that out of Lloyds. Ask for £5,000. and you'll get it all' (fund-raisers take note). We did and the cross and candelabras became a memorial to members of Lloyds who had served at sea during the war. Some years ago, I know not when, they were removed for so-called security reasons. Somebody did the thieves' work for them. I grieved at their removal and the substitution of a woefully inadequate wooden replacement. Cross and Candlesticks were as the keystone of the arch. Their strength and beauty focussed the eyes and the larger understanding. They were the raison d'etre and the crowning expression of a man-sized religion.

They symbolised what the Archbishop was saying about sacrifice; about the best in life being achieved at cost. 'Whosoever does not bear his cross and come after me cannot be my disciple.' It is that challenge which is proclaimed from pulpit and altar. The more impressive both are, the clearer they should speak and draw out from each of us our response to that Gospel. Respond we must to the privilege of bearing the Cross of whatever sort it may be. It differs for each of us but just as surely is laid on all. And we learn at the Altar how to bear it as we identify with Christ in his triumphant sacrifice.

Pray God that this Chapel will always, in all its magnificent beauty, tell out the greatness and the majesty of the Lord so that we are moved to respond to Him in sacrifice — at cost to ourselves — who of His love gave His life for us.

THE WEDNESDAY ROSTRUM

It took me about a year to evolve a proper evangelistic routine for Guild Church activity in St Lawrence Jewry. What was to become significant over the next 15 years was the series of talks given during the lunch hour on a Wednesday: a day when politicians would not be tied to Westminster for Prime Minister's Questions, and free to come to us. Many did.

Appendixes

I saw the talks as part of the traditional role played by St Lawrence Jewry over the centuries. At the time of the Renaissance, Sir Thomas More, who lived just over the road in Milk Street, encouraged by the then Vicar, Dr Grocyn, thought out his position which he expressed later in his Utopia as he discussed St Augustine's City of God. Towards the end of the 17th century, the Enlightment, John Tillotson (soon to become Archbishop of Canterbury) and many of the other distinguished thinkers of the age were encouraged to come by the Rector, Dr John Wilkins, a co-founder of the Royal Society.

It was my good fortune to be able to get the Rt Hon J Enoch Powell to give the first talks on the 11, 18 and 25 May 1971: they were later published in his book 'No Easy Answers'. He spoke to packed churches; pews, chairs and standing room were all fully occupied. This flourishing start gave us publicity in the City and set a standard. They were seen as occasions for a meeting of minds: with thinkers and those who had social responsibilities and leadership in various activities. There followed, among others (as they were then): Malcolm Muggeridge: Chay Blyth: Ernest Shippam: Lord Robens: Leonard Cheshire: William Deedes: Jack Dash: Sam Wanamaker: Bishop Trevor Huddleston: Ross McWhirter: Hardiman Scott: Mary Whitehouse: Richard Gilbert Scott: David Hemery: Frederick Catherwood: Dick Taverne: Lord Watkinson: Sir Geoffrey Jackson: John Hefferman: Donald Swann: Jack Ashley: Bernard Miles: Andrew Cruickshank.

Thereafter, I felt that the talks had become so much a feature of our life at St Lawrence Jewry, that I organised courses on selected themes. The pattern over the year became, in broad terms: Lent (Spring) Faith; Summer — Charity, the Arts Sportsmanship; and, in the Autumn — Morality and the City.

And so, hundreds each week, sometimes to the limits that safety regulations allowed, had their minds stretched and felt privileged to see and hear, without the bias of the media, and to meet and question people with known expertise or carrying special responsibilities in national life. Many who attended have expressed their thanks either verbally or in writing. I was, on the other hand, given quite a bit of stick for seemingly only inviting the political Right. There have, in fact, been few people in the headlines whom I did not ask, the few being obvious perpetrators of double-speak: some, for various reasons, declined. In 1974 after he had sent his flying pickets to disrupt George Ward, who was speaking on Grunwick, I asked Mr Scargill. His reply: 'My dear Vicar, you must realise that I am a very busy man: Yours.

The Rt. Hon. J Enoch Powell MBE. He began the sequence of Wednesday Talks, the first of many given between May 1971 and July 1986, listed on pages 180–185. He spoke almost annually always to a packed church — standing room only. *Photograph by courtesy of The Daily Telegraph.*

Appendixes

etc.' I am sure that he does not mind me revealing that now. But I have had my own standards of propriety in these matters and never felt that I should divulge the refusals — why should they come in any case? How good they were to do so. The ultimate accolade was accorded us, even though in jest, by the Governor of the Bank of England: 'To be known to have spoken on the platform in St Lawrence Jewry is the equivalent of a mention in Crockford for having preached the University Sermon!'

I was careful about asking people to speak from a rostrum, not from the pulpit. I also pointed out that they would be subject to questions, possibly heckling. (That was bad enough to have to request police assistance on four occasions). A rostrum implies an exchange of views: a pulpit, the proclamation of the Gospel. Church architecture and ornaments are liturgical: they express by position and structure what Christians believe about themselves and their activity. I don't believe that the pulpit should be trivialised as a convenient place from which to make announcements or to conduct choirs or prayers. That indicates the loss of Faith by the contemporary Church in what it is supposed to proclaim. The pulpit in St Lawrence Jewry was reserved for preaching; and the rostrum rigged for dialogue, teaching, catechism. Intellectual standards were high. I shall never forget the awed respect with which people automatically stood when Mr Enoch Powell stepped off the platform for the last time. There was no applause as was the norm, but looks of amazement on their faces as they contemplated the brilliance and eloquence to which they had been treated by him and so many others. Silence was a mark of their sadness that such talks had come to an end. He had very kindly given the talks such a fair wind in 1971 and had returned some five or six times over the years. He ended them with a flourish in 1986: and with thanks from the hundreds who came to us on Wednesdays as well as from me.

THE WEDNESDAY ROSTRUM PROGRAM

God and my Health
June/July 1974
    Dr Beric Wright
    Dr James Watson
    Prof. Desmond Pond
    Dr John L Cox
    Prof. Linford Rees
    Archie Hill

For Such a Time as This
Oct./Nov. 1974
    Sir John Donaldson
    Ralph Harris
    Robin Page
    Sir Geoffrey Howe
    Brian Faulkner PC
    J Enoch Powell

Appendixes

Mrs Thatcher. Young Communist demonstrators, of whom there were numbers in various parts of the church, had to be led out by the police. This was one of four such organized interruptions of selected talks. *Photograph by courtesy of The Times.*

Remoralising Britain
Feb./March 1975
    Lord George-Brown
    Gen. Sir Walter Walker
    Ronald Butt
    The Earl of Cromer
    Dr Rhodes Boyson
    The Revd. Dr Kenneth Slack

My Hope for the Future
June/July 1975
    Sir Christopher Soames
    Frank Chapple
    Lord Chalfont
    Lord Elton
    Ross McWhirter
    Bp. Trevor Huddleston

Money and Morality
Jan./Feb. 1976
    David Malbert
    Dominick Harrod
    Nigel Lawson
    Patrick Hutber
    Kenneth Fleet
    Frances Cairncross

Death
Jan./Feb. 1976
    Chllr E Garth Moore
    Dr C M Parkes
    Dr Cicely Saunders
    Dr Una Kroll
    Bp. of Salisbury
    Bp. of Southwark

Appendixes

A Ross McWhirter Tribute
May/June 1976
   Lord de L'Isle VC
   Dr Rhodes Boyson
   Ralph Harris
   Michael Thomas QC
   Winston Churchill
   Norris McWhirter

Social Responsibility
Oct./Nov 1976
   A G C Trollope
   John Hargreaves
   Edmund de Rothschild
   H H T Hudson
   F F Wolff
   Rt Hon Lord Armstrong
   Basil Fehr
   Nicholas Goodison

Patriotism
Jan./Feb. 1977
   J Enoch Powell
   HE The Israeli Ambassador
   Sir Monty Finniston
   Sir Derek Ezra
   Eric Heffer
   Sir Geoffrey Jackson

Listening to Music
April/May 1977
   Steve Race
   John Kentish
   Sir Charles Groves CBE
   Anthony Hopkins
   Col. Paul Neville MVO FRAM
   Richard Rodney Bennett
   Malcolm Williamson CBE

A Jubilee Series
June/July 1977
   Lord George Brown
   John Gouriet
   Reg. Prentice
   Jane Ewart Biggs
   Michael Brotherton
   Tom Fleming

Russian Communism and Christian Order
Oct./Nov. 1977
   George Ward
   Robert Moss
   Vladimir Bukovsky
   Lord Chalfont
   Dr Rhodes Boyson
   Ralph Harris
   Brian Griffiths

Education: the Great Debate
Feb./March 1978
   Ruth Garwood-Scott OBE
   Prof. Charles Rowley
   C Everett MA
   Mrs Mary Whitehouse
   Prof. Anthony Flew
   Prof. Julius Gould

Medicine and Ethics
April/May 1978
   Prof. J P Watson
   Dr Patricia W Gillan
   Ian Kennedy LL M
   Prof. R M Hare
   Rev. Michael Day
   Dr Max Glatt

Charity
June 1978
   David Jacobs
   Brian Rix
   Susan Hampshire

Church and Organ Music
Sept./Oct. 1978
   Christopher Dearnley
   Colin Mawby
   Noel Mander
   Margaret Phillips
   Stephen Dykes Bower

Appendixes

I Believe
November 1978
  John Biggs-Davison, MP
  Arianna Stassinopoulos
  Peter Brooke, MP
  George Ward
  Tariq Ali

The Defence of the Realm
Jan./Feb. 1979
  Gp. Capt. Leonard
  Cheshire, VC
  Sir Neil Cameron, GCB
  Winston Churchill, MP
  Brian Crozier
  Robert Moss
  Lord Chalfont, PC
  Peter Walker, PC MP

Transcendental Meditation
May 1979
  Dr Roger Graham

Comparative Religions
May 1979
  Shaikh Muhammad Tufail
  Mr Christmas Humphreys
  Mr Moshe Davis
  Dr F A Chandra

Trade Unionism
June/July 1979
  George Ward
  Tom Chapman
  Lord George Brown
  Lord Caldecote
  Jack Peel
  John Cousins

Charity
Oct./Nov. 1979
  Edward Fox
  Angharad Rees &
  Christopher Cazenove
  Monty Modlyn
  Judith Chalmers
  Sir Ian Gourlay
  Charles Maugham

Law Order and Society
November 1979
  Rev. Charles Curran
  Rev. John Coventry SJ
  J E S Fawcett

Readings
Jan./Feb. 1980
  Lady Wilson
  Lord Bernard Miles
  Roy Fuller
  Robert Dougall
  John Julius Norwich

Spirituality
Feb./March./April 1980
  Archbp. Anthony of Sourozh
  The Revd. Richard Harries
  The Revd. Dr Howard Williams
  The Mother Superior General
  All Saints Covent, Oxford
  The Revd. Father Michael Hollings
  The Revd. Dr E S Abbott KCVO

Our Daily Bread
April/May 1980
  Winston Churchill MP
  Arthur Seldon
  The Rt. Hon Peter Shore MP
  Sir Henry Plumb
  The Rt. Hon Lord George-Brown

The Arts
June/July 1980
  Lady Solti
  Viscount Eccles
  Bryan Jefferson
  Terence Cuneo

The Family: Its Supervision
Oct./Nov. 1980
  Mary Whitehouse
  Valerie Riches

Appendixes

Eddy Stride
Mary Kenny
Jill Knight MP
Raymond Johnson

The Spirit of the Nation
March/April 1981
    The Rt. Hon Margaret Thatcher MP
    Nicholas Goodison
    Sir Larry Lamb
    Sir David McNee QPM
    Walter Goldsmith
    Rear Adml. Edward Gueritz CB OBE DSC
    The Rt. Hon J Enoch Powell MBE MP

Sovereignty
May/June 1981
    Dr. A L Rowse
    Norris McWhirter
    T E Utley
    Timothy Raison MP
    Msgr. Ralph Brown

Sportsmanship
Oct./Nov. 1981
    James Hunt
    Dorian Williams
    Virginia Wade
    Christopher Martin-Jenkins
    Stan Smith
    John Young

Lent
1982
    Dr A L Rowse
    James McMillan
    Keith Wickenden MP
    Pat Lowry
    David Hopkinson
    Sir John Boyd
    The Rt. Hon Norman Tebbit MP

The Price of Peace
Oct./Nov. 1982
    The Rt. Hon J Enoch Powell MBE MP
    Brian Crozier

Ray Whitney MP
Lt. Gen. Steuart Pringle Bt
The Bishop of London
The Rt. Hon Lord Chalfont
The Rt. Hon John Nott MP

Charity
June 1983
    Pete Murray
    Claire Oberman
    Brian Rix
    Dr Magnus Pyke
    Max Hastings

Hope
Oct./Nov. 1983
    Lady Oppenheimer
    Sir Keith Joseph Bt MP
    Stephen O'Brien
    Ivan Fallon
    The Rt. Hon The Lord Home
    of the Hirsel
    Dr Rhodes Boyson MP
    Archbishop Lord Coggan

Lent
1984
    The Rt. Hon J Enoch Powell MBE MP
    David Kossoff Esq
    The Rt. Hon Viscount Tonypandy

The Morality of the Creation of Wealth
Oct./Nov. 1984
    Sir Nigel Broackes
    The Lord Rayner
    Ian MacGregor Esq
    Robin Leigh-Pemberton Esq
    Clive Thornton Esq
    John Egan Esq
    Sir Peter Walters

Alternative Medicine
May 1985
    Michael van Stratten Esq
    Matthew Manning Esq

Appendixes

Miss Caroline Saulder
Dr Pietroni

The Morality of the Distribution of Wealth
Oct./Nov. 1985
  Geoffrey Owen Esq
  Sir Hector Laing
  The Rt. Hon Lord Young
  The Rt. Hon Lord Seebohm
  The Rt. Hon Lord Bauer
  Prof. Brian Griffiths

My Faith and Contemporary Life
Feb./March 1986
  John Selwyn Gummer MP
  The Cardinal Archbp. of Westminster
  Peter Utley Esq
  Sir Richard Acland
  Mrs Mary Whitehouse
  Lady Olga Maitland
  The Rt. Hon J Enoch Powell MBE MP

Epilogue

THE BANQUET

He was known to them in the breaking of the Bread.
St Luke, Chap. 24 v 35.

My life must be Christ's broken bread
My love his outpoured wine
A cup o'er filled, a table spread
Beneath His Name and Sign
That other souls refreshed and fed
May share His Life through mine.

Albert Osborn

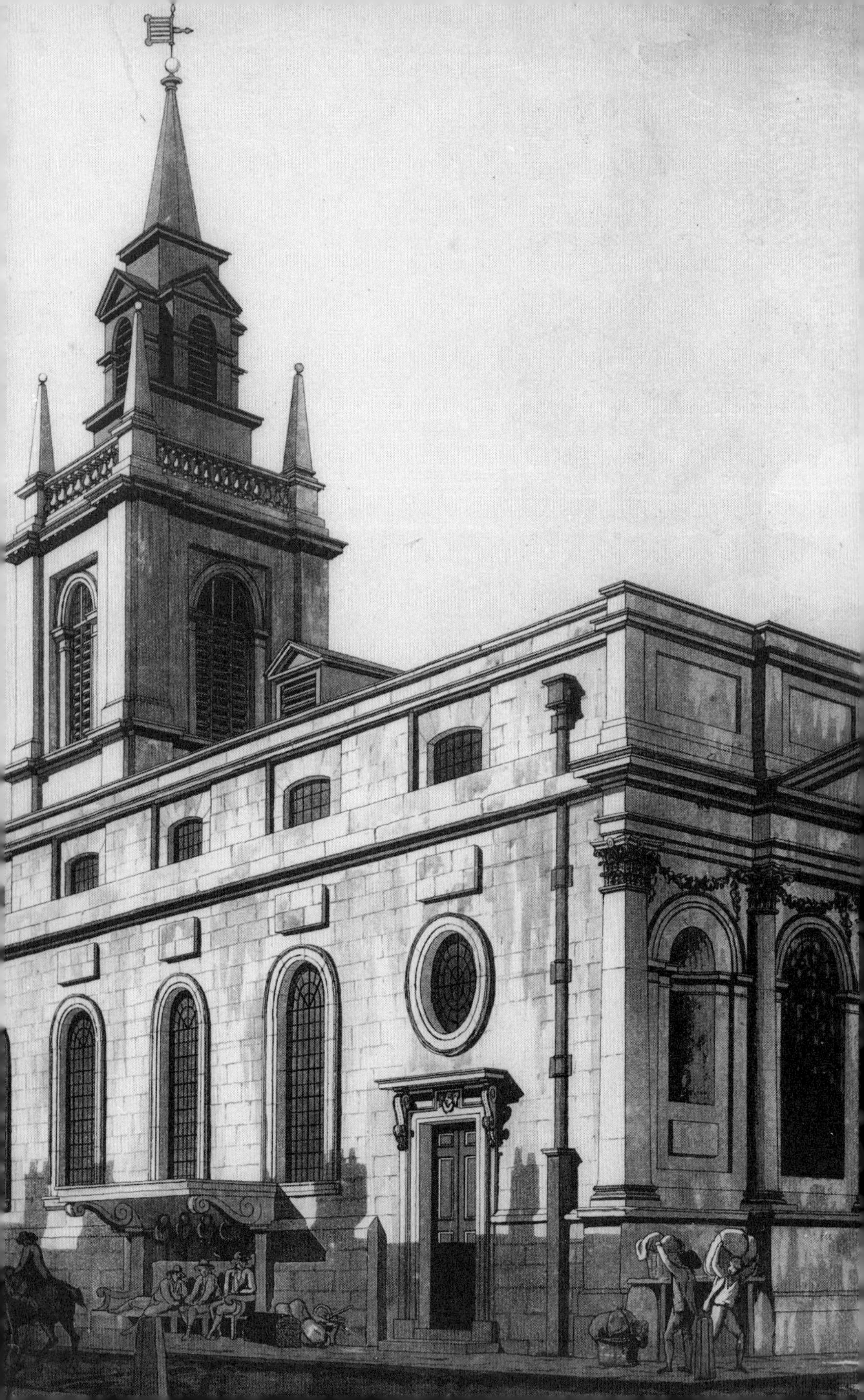